ISBN 978-1-330-42489-6
PIBN 10060841

1 MONTH OF
FREE
READING

at

www.ForgottenBooks.com

By purchasing this book you are eligible for one month membership to ForgottenBooks.com, giving you unlimited access to our entire collection of over 1,000,000 titles via our web site and mobile apps.

To claim your free month visit:

www.forgottenbooks.com/free60841

English
Français
Deutsche
Italiano
Español
Português

www.forgottenbooks.com

Mythology Photography **Fiction**
Fishing Christianity **Art** Cooking
Essays Buddhism Freemasonry
Medicine **Biology** Music **Ancient
Egypt** Evolution Carpentry Physics
Dance Geology **Mathematics** Fitness
Shakespeare **Folklore** Yoga Marketing
Confidence Immortality Biographies
Poetry **Psychology** Witchcraft
Electronics Chemistry History **Law**
Accounting **Philosophy** Anthropology
Alchemy Drama Quantum Mechanics
Atheism Sexual Health **Ancient History**
Entrepreneurship Languages Sport
Paleontology Needlework Islam
Metaphysics Investment Archaeology
Parenting Statistics Criminology
Motivational

The Religion of the Church

AS PRESENTED IN THE CHURCH OF ENGLAND

A Manual of Membership

By CHARLES GORE, D.D.

Bishop of Oxford

A. R. MOWBRAY & CO. LTD.
LONDON: 28 Margaret Street, Oxford Circus, W.
OXFORD: 9 High Street
MILWAUKEE, U.S.A.: THE YOUNG CHURCHMAN CO.

First impression, September, 1916
New impression, October, 1916

PREFACE

THIS little book is intended as a summary statement of the religion of the catholic church. It is intended to meet a need, which is just now clamorous—the provision of a manual of instruction for the members of the Church of England. It has been rapidly written, and, from the nature of the case, can supply little in the way of proofs or justifications of its statements. But I can truthfully plead that there is nothing here written down that has not behind it the meditation and study of a lifetime ; and in other books I have sought to supply the grounds, or a great part of the grounds, on which the statements of this book repose. I hope my critics will remember this.

My little book has had the advantage of the very careful criticisms and suggestions of Father Paul Bull, C.R. I have not seen my way to accept all his suggestions, and he has no responsibility for what appears in the book. But the help he has given me has been invaluable. I owe to the Rev. Wilfrid Cooper, my chaplain, the short index to the topics treated in the book.

C. OXON:

Michaelmas, 1916.

NOTE

I have been several times asked why I do not print such words as Church, Sacrament, Precious Blood, etc., with a capital. There are, I suppose, two principles on which capitals may be used. One principle, which seems to be dominant, is to use them, even in the case of adjectives, to express sacredness or dignity or importance. The other principle, the principle of the English Bible, is to use them only for proper names. I greatly prefer this principle, and seek to adhere to it, save that I have not dared (except in quotations from the Bible) to print the personal pronouns referring to God without the capitals. Otherwise, I desire to adhere to the principle of the English Bible. I suppose "Church of England," "Church of Rome," "the Pope," "the Archbishop of Canterbury" to be proper names requiring capitals. Otherwise, I print church, bishop, etc., without a capital. It does not seem to me to matter much. But one likes to have some principle to adhere to, and I think the best principle is, as far as possible, to reserve capitals for proper names.

CONTENTS

THE RELIGION OF THE CHURCH

※※

CHAPTER I

Membership in the Church

CHRISTIANITY is a certain kind of personal belief and a certain kind of personal life ; but it is not a merely individual religion, "a private matter between a man's soul and God." It is membership, with all the responsibility of membership, in a society or brother-hood which Jesus Christ our Lord founded to bind together in one men of all classes and races and kinds. This society is the Holy Catholic Church, and the Church of England is a part of the catholic church.

Read the Gospels, and you will read of Jesus Christ founding His church and giving to it and to its officers authority

B

over all its members, authority to "bind"
and "loose"[1]—that is to prohibit this and
to allow that—with a divine sanction ; and
authority to "remit" and "retain" sins[2]
with divine ratification—that is to admit
men into its fellowship or to exclude
them if they are unworthy, and to readmit
them when they show themselves penitent.
Years before our present Gospels were
written down, the Christian church was
acting on this commission. Read the First
Epistle of S. Paul to the Corinthians and
you will find a vivid account of one of
the first Christian churches. There is
plenty of sin and wilfulness to be found
there, but there is no mistaking the
intense sense of membership. They had
been brought at their baptism by the one
Spirit into the one body, and they celebrated together the Holy Communion, the
sacrament of continual membership. The
authority of the whole body and of the
apostle is asserted and acknowledged over
every member. Any plainly unworthy
member is to be judged and excluded
from their company "in the name of
the Lord Jesus," and one so excluded,
when he is penitent, can be received back
into communion or forgiven "in the

[1] S. Matt. xvi. 19; xviii 18.
[2] S. John xx. 23.

person of Christ."[1] Every member is expected to take a part and interest in the affairs of the church, its discipline, and its worship. For a "member" means a limb, and every limb of the body has to do part of the work of the body. And as they had learned from Christ the infinite worth of every human soul, so in their fellowship they recognized that the need of each is the care of all, and that "if one member suffer, all the members suffer with it." The great salvation in which they all rejoiced was a gift of God for all which bound them into brotherhood: and they acted on the principle of all true brotherhood—"from each according to his capacity: to each according to his need." Many things promoted the growth of the church in early days—the steadfast faith of Christians, the high moral level of their lives, the courage and joy with which they faced trouble or death ; but, perhaps more than all else, it was the intense sense of membership, the spirit of mutual love, which drew men to them. And every local church in every age has been either an effective or an ineffective part of the body of Christ, just in proportion as the sense of member-

[1] See for the whole of this paragraph 1 Cor. xii ; 1 Cor. x. 15–22 ; 1 Cor. v ; 2 Cor. ii. 5–11, etc.

ship and the responsibility of membership
has been strong or weak.

When you come down the history of
the church to the Church of England,
as it was re-ordered at the Reformation,
and read its Book of Common Prayer,
you will see that it meant to maintain at
a very high level the responsibility of
membership. Those who are to be baptized are to recognize publicly before
the congregation assembled their responsibility for renouncing what Christ forbids,
for believing the common faith of the
church, and for obeying the laws of
discipleship. They are embarking, and
that publicly, on a great adventure, and
they must know what they are doing. If
infants are to be baptized, then sponsors
must be provided as sureties, to guarantee
that the infants, as they grow to years of
discretion, shall know the meaning of their
religion. And they are to renew the vows
of baptism through their own lips before
they can be confirmed, by the laying-on
of the bishop's hand, and so enter upon
full membership in the strength of the
Holy Spirit. The Lord's Supper or Holy
Communion is the sacrament in which
their membership is to be constantly
renewed and reinvigorated, and it is to
be guarded by the officers of the church

from unworthy partaking. Those whose
lives cause public scandal are to be
warned or, if need be, excommunicated,
or put out of fellowship, till they have
shown themselves of a better mind, and
"been openly reconciled by penance,"
and so can be readmitted to fellowship.
And private confession and absolution is
provided for those whose conscience is
troubled by secret sins. And the needs
of the poor and sick are to be relieved
by the alms of the whole community.
And the law of indissoluble marriage
is to set its consecration upon the home.
And the sick and dying are to be dealt
with as responsible members who must
be brought to a right faith and penitence, and make their peace with God
and man, that, if they die, the words
of confident hope, such as belong rightly
to the holy fellowship of the church,
may be spoken over their graves.

All this is natural and right. Every
union or society which exists for any
worthy object must maintain a high sense
of the responsibility of membership ; and
all its members must recognize that, if
they fail to keep its obligatory rules, they
must fall out of membership and lose its
advantages. A nominal membership is the
curse of any union. What trade union

could last if a large percentage of its members never obeyed its rules or ful-filled their obligations?

But if this is true, then indeed we know wherein lies the present weakness of the Church of England. It has cheapened membership till it has come to mean almost nothing. Of our soldiers we are told seventy per cent. recognize them-selves as members of the Church of England, but it is only a small number whose membership has meant much in their lives. The sacrament of continual fellowship has been ignored. They have taken no interest in the affairs of the church. They have never been led to think of the management of the church as if it was their business. They have not felt it as a fellowship. It has not led them to expect that if they were wronged or unjustly treated, it would be the duty and privilege of the church to see them righted. They have the vaguest idea of the church's faith, and a very weak sense of either the joy or the responsibility of common worship. They have no idea that they wrong the church by evil living, or that the church has anything to do with the matter. For old associations' sake they like to be married in church, and to bring their

children to be christened, and to send
their children to the Sunday school, and
they wish to be buried with the church's
service. But for the rest, membership
in the church means almost nothing.
Now I have no doubt at all that the
reform which is the most fundamental and
necessary, if there is to be any effectual
revival of religion in our old Church
of England, is to recover the feeling of
the obligations of membership. What we
want first of all is not more Christians but
better Christians, not more Churchmen
but better Churchmen. Every one must
understand that he or she cannot become
or remain a member of the church without fulfilling the elementary responsibilities
of membership. All Christians are called
"kings and priests" in the New Testament,
and they should exercise their kingship and
priesthood by active participation in the
affairs and worship of the church. Both
their duties and their rights need to be
much more fully recognized. A vast
change is needed in this direction. But
the first step is to revive the sense of
membership; and because I believe this to
be the most fundamental and necessary of
all reforms, I have called this book, which
attempts to explain the religion of the
church according to the use and practice

of the Church of England, a "manual of
membership."

The church has lately had it brought
home to it how small a proportion of "the
workers" are practising Churchmen.   At
the same time the ideas and aspirations
of brotherhood—that is, the spirit of
mutual membership—are stirring the world
of labour to its depths.   There is, I am
persuaded, only one way in which the
church can commend its message to labour.
It is not by lowering its doctrine or cheapen-
ing its claim.   It is by making the spirit of
brotherhood, the spirit of mutual membership, once again real and effective in the
church, which indeed was founded to
carry into every corner of the earth the
witness of Christ to the worth and dignity
of every human being for whom Christ
died.

CHAPTER II

The Catholic Faith

THREE preliminaries must first be considered.

1. *The religion of the church is based upon a word (or revelation) of God.*—The people of Israel was called by God among ancient peoples to be His people and to reveal His "name" and purpose among men. In the words of a great Christian father the Jews were, through their prophets, "the sacred school of the knowledge of God and of the spiritual life for all mankind." The Jews were thus the ancient and preparatory church of God. The church of Jesus Christ took its origin out of this ancient church, but it is catholic or universal, a super-national fellowship, based upon the fuller revelation of God which is given us in Jesus Christ. But the Jewish church and the church of Christ are really one church, and are alike based on the word of God— that is, on God's revelation of Himself given first through His prophets and then finally through His Son: and to become,

9   C

or remain rightly, a member of the
church each one must accept the message
of the church—its fundamental faith—as
being truly "the word of God." There
are solemn words of our Lord which sound
strangely in our ears: "I thank thee, Father,
Lord of heaven and earth, that thou didst
hide these things (that is, His message)
from the wise and understanding, and didst
reveal them unto babes: yea, Father, for
so it was well-pleasing in thy sight. All
things have been delivered unto me of
my Father: and no one knoweth the Son
save the Father, neither doth any know
the Father save the Son and he to whomsoever the Son willeth to reveal him."[1]
In this wonderful saying our Lord asserts
His own community of nature with God
His Father, and His unique claim to reveal
God to men; and He expresses a positive
joy in the fact that while the learned refuse
His message the simple accept it. He sees
in this the fulfilment of a divine purpose,
and S. Paul after Him, in different words,
does the same thing. A little thought will
enable us to understand our Lord's joy in
what would at first sight seem to us to have
been a grave disaster. It is that only so
could a really broad and enduring church

[1] S. Matt. xi. 25-27; S. Luke x. 21, 22; 1 Cor. i.
18-31.

be founded or propagated. The learned, the intellectuals, of every age, instinctively claim the prerogative of their learning. They are, in this respect, like rich men who also instinctively expect a prerogative position because they are rich; whom, therefore, our Lord similarly treated as being under a special disadvantage in their approach to His kingdom. What is the claim made commonly by a learned class? It is that they will only accept as true what commends itself to them as the con- clusion of their own reasonings. But the intellectual methods and principles of learned men are not commonly intel- ligible to the mass of ordinary men, and also vary considerably, even profoundly, from age to age and nation to nation. Thus a religion which in any age should approve itself to the learned class as the conclusion of its own reasoning would be a narrow religion, unacceptable to the mass of men and still more unacceptable to men of another nation or another civilization. If there is to be a catholic church, a religion for the common man, all the world over and in every generation, it must be based not on human reasoning but on divine revelation, on God's disclosure of Himself, and must be received by men in simple faith as God's own word. Our religion

is not to be an evolution from within, but
a bestowal from above ; not a conclusion
of logic, but a gift of God; to be welcomed
on authority and then verified in experience — our own experience fortified and
supported by the experience of the whole
church. That is what the Bible says,
and truly, both Old Testament and New :
"Canst thou by searching find out God?
Canst thou find out the Almighty unto
perfection? It is high as heaven; what
canst thou do? Deeper than the grave;
what canst thou know?" "In the wisdom
of God the world through its wisdom knew
not God." "Hath not God made foolish
the wisdom of the world?"[1] That is the
claim of the Christian faith. A brilliant
scientist, like Louis Pasteur, may be a
devout Christian, but that is because, like
Pasteur, he has been content in the first
instance to receive his faith, like the most
ignorant person, as the word of God from
the church which is commissioned to
bear it.

2. *The purpose of this book is to expound
this word of God.*—To receive the message
of Christ from His church in simple
docility a man must be convinced that
Jesus Christ really is the Son of God, and
has really sent His church into the world.

[1] Job xi. 7, 8 ; 1 Cor. i. 20, 21.

In one who comes from outside this conviction will be brought about in one case
mostly by intellectual, in another case
mostly by moral considerations, in another
case by personal influence. To produce
this preliminary intellectual conviction is
the work of what is called "apologetics"—
that is, the reasoned expression of the
grounds of Christian belief. In this book
I am not concerned with that. I assume
in my readers that they are so far convinced, or willing to be convinced, about
Christ either by tradition from their
fathers, or by intellectual reasonings, or
by their moral needs, as to be ready to
listen with docile hearts to the message
of "grace and truth which came by Jesus
Christ." My duty is to make it plain that
the message claims to be based, not on
human reason, but on a divine revelation
given us finally in Jesus Christ; and my
business is to explain the points and articles
of this message, as the church, which is
Christ's commissioned agent, delivered it
from the first. Personal faith is a gift—
a priceless gift—wrought in the heart by
the Spirit of God: "No man can say,
Jesus is Lord, but in the Holy Spirit."
But an important part of the preparation
of our hearts for this gift is to be ready
to listen attentively and patiently to what

the message is.   To reject it or despise it without having really been at pains to understand what it is, after all that the message of the Gospel has done for the world, is a sort of insolence.

3. *The word of God must be looked for in the first instance from the church.*—The church was at work perhaps some twenty years before any of the books of the New Testament, as we now have them, were written, and some seventy years before they were all written.   It will not surprise us, therefore, to find out that no one of the books of the New Testament was written to give to any one his first instruction in the Christian religion. "That thou mayest know the certainty of those things *in which thou wast instructed*" is the object with which St. Luke wrote his Gospel.   And when S. Paul writes in his Epistle to the Corinthians about the resurrection or the eucharist it is to remind them of "the gospel which I preached unto you, which also ye received." "For I delivered unto you first of all that which also I received."   That is the tone of the whole New Testament.   It assumes and takes for granted the rudimentary instruction which had been already given to the converts to the church.   Speaking generally, we may say that all that is con-

tained in our catechism is, in the New Testament, taken for granted as already familiar ground among the Christians. And the different books of the New Testament were written as occasion arose by the apostles or their companions to record the tradition in its best form, or to reinforce and explain and defend the fundamental faith. It is thus the function of "the church to teach and of the Bible to prove" and confirm the faith. And so complete are the books of Scripture taken together, and so full the inspiration of the Spirit of God under which they were believed to have been written, that it became the accepted principle of the catholic church from the first, as it still is of the Church of England, that nothing could be part of the necessary faith but what can be verified and proved in Scripture. "Do not believe what I say simply," says a great teacher of the early church to his scholars preparing for baptism, "unless you receive the proof of what I tell you from the Holy Scriptures."[1]

With these preliminaries I propose to give a summary of the faith of the church, which is also the faith of the New Testament Scriptures.

[1] S. Cyril of Jerusalem, *Catechetical Lectures*, iv. 17.

CHAPTER III

The Doctrine of God and of His Creatures

THE centre and root of the catholic faith is the revelation of the Fatherhood of God—the doctrine that the one power which made and preserves and guides the whole universe is the almighty will of a perfectly good God, who creates and knows and loves not only all but each.

THE FATHERHOOD OF GOD

Welcome as it is to the hearts of men, this is perhaps the hardest of all Christian doctrines to the speculative intellect. It is so hard to reconcile with the facts of suffering and injustice and cruelty, and with the seeming moral indifference of nature. The intellect of man would never have attained securely to this position by mere inquiry and investigation. It rests on God's own revelation of Himself—a revelation given specially through a long succession

16

of Jewish prophets who were inspired to proclaim as the word of God the goodness of the Almighty,[1] and it received its final expression through the lips of one who was more than a prophet, who was the Son of God—who therefore not only proclaimed the truth, and claimed the right to declare it with infallible certitude, but also, as incarnate in our manhood, disclosed to us the real character and mind of God in the intelligible terms of a human life.

Our Lord was always bringing home to the minds and hearts of men the truth of God's fatherhood, His universal and individual love. Consider the following characteristic sayings: "It is not the will of your Father which is in heaven that one of these little ones should perish." "Not a sparrow shall fall on the ground without your Father: fear ye not therefore, ye are of more value than many sparrows." "Your Father knoweth what things ye have need of before ye ask him." "Your heavenly Father knoweth that ye have need of all these things." And He claims to speak with infallible assurance—"No one knoweth the Father save the Son,

---

[1] The word "Almighty" or "omnipotent" means properly not so much "able to do all things" as "powerful in and over all things"—the all-ruler.

and he to whomsoever the Son willeth
to reveal Him "—and not only to reveal
in words, but in His own person to express
God. "He that hath seen me hath seen
the Father." Such sayings abound in the
Gospels, and are the centre of our Lord's
teaching. They are best summarized in
the great sentence of S. John, "God is
love."

It is an amazing paradox. And there is
no question that what made it believable
was that it was revealed in full view of all
the experience which makes it seem so
paradoxical. The Old Testament revelation of the one good God was given in a
blood-stained world that was being trampled
by the feet of fierce conquering armies—
Assyrians and Egyptians, Babylonians and
Persians, who neither showed nor expected any mercy. It was given to a
weak and enslaved people—the Israelites
in captivity—who knew all that bitter
experience can teach. And when the
Lord Jesus Christ expressed and deepened
and expanded the doctrine, it was as "the
man of sorrows and acquainted with
grief," who in His own person endured
everything that has ever been an argument against the divine love, everything
that in slow and embittering experience
has ever soured the hearts of men, and

turned philanthropists into cynics. He
held and proclaimed the mighty truth even
from the cross of failure and shame, on
which He asked the great question, "My
God, my God, why didst thou forsake
me?" And His resurrection the third
day from the dead was God's vindication
of Him; the central evidence in one signi-
ficant act that the power of God, the one
power which made and rules the world, is
through all seeming weakness and failure
on the side of Jesus of Nazareth.

These, then, are the attributes of God
which it is always most important to have
in mind.

1. *Omnipotence*—which means that the
one all-creating and all-pervading power,
which is both in the whole universe and
over it, inexhaustible and eternal, is the
sovereign will of God, who can do all
things which are in accordance with His
own nature and purpose. He has willed
to create free beings, and therefore tol-
erates all the confusion which their rebellion has introduced into the world,
but He is yet in His supreme wisdom
guiding all things to a conclusion, an
" end of the world," in which He will
vindicate Himself in His whole creation. Thus from the truth of God's
almightiness follows the confident ex-

pectation of the Day of the Lord, of
which we hear so much in the Bible,
when God at last is to come into His
own in the person of Jesus Christ His
Son ; "whereof he hath given assurance
unto all men, in that he hath raised him
from the dead."

2. *Righteousness.* The special characteristic of the whole Bible is its insistence on
the character of God—that He is absolutely
righteous and holy, and claims of all free
beings whom He has created a like
righteousness in their relation to Him
and to one another; and is to be pro-
pitiated by no gifts or sacrifices or ceremonies, but only by conformity with His
own character; and has impressed a witness
to His righteousness upon the consciences
of men, who thereby know themselves to
be under God's righteous judgement; and
has enlightened their conscience by the
teaching of His prophets and His Son,
through His Holy Spirit.

3. *Love.* The tremendous severity of
the divine righteousness must always
cause men to fear Him with a holy fear.
But the perfection of righteousness is
love. And finally, in the revelation of
Jesus Christ the Son, the ultimate nature
of God is disclosed as pure goodness—such
that He loves every creature that He has

created, and intends nothing but good for every one, and is afflicted in every one's affliction, and shrinks from no sacrifice in order to redeem, and will one day manifest His sovereign love in the whole universe.

What more about the nature of God is expressed in His revelation of His heart towards man will appear when we come to speak of the Holy Trinity.

JESUS CHRIST

It has already appeared how God revealed Himself at last through His own and only-begotten Son, Jesus Christ our Lord. Him men saw and heard as man among men, and they came to believe in Him first as prophet, then as the Christ of God, and then as His eternal Son or Word incarnate. The process of this belief is apparent in the New Testament, and its conclusion found expression in the Creeds. The belief of the church, then, which is confirmed in the New Testament, is that Jesus Christ is the eternal Son of God, "very God of very God," that is "of one substance with the Father;" by whom all things were made and are sustained in being; who for us men and for our salvation was, in the fullness of time, made man by a human birth, through the power of the

Holy Ghost, in the womb of the blessed
virgin Mary; so that He was born "perfect God and perfect man," differing in
His manhood from other men in that He
was sinless—God's new creation; true
man in all that properly belongs to humanity, but new man—the second Adam,
free from all the taint and hindrance of
sin. In this our manhood, in the power
of the Holy Spirit, He lived and taught
and gathered disciples and founded His
church: in this manhood He was rejected, and suffered and was crucified: upon
the cross He truly died, and His dead
body was laid in the grave, while His
spirit went where all human spirits go—
to hell, or Hades, the place of the dead,
where He preached His gospel to the dead
also: and on the third day, by the power
of God, He was raised from the dead—not
resuscitated to His old manner of life, but
transformed in His bodily nature into the
condition of the "spiritual body," a state
of existence which S. Paul declares to
be the destiny of us all.[1] In this risen
body He appeared to His disciples during
forty days for the confirmation of their
faith and for their further instruction,
and mounted out of their sight by an
ascension above the clouds which repre-

[1] See later, pp. 82–87.

sented to their eyes the spiritual truth
of His assumption to the throne of all the
world, whence He shall come again in the
final Day of the Lord to be the judge of
quick and dead.

These events in our Lord's human life
which have fallen within the scope of
human experience can be expressed in
literal human language. Thus He truly
was born of the Virgin, and truly died,
and truly after His resurrection appeared
to His disciples and ascended to heaven.
But, so far as concerns what lies outside human experience, what concerns
His going to the place of departed spirits,
or hell, and His "sitting in heaven at the
right hand of God," we can only use
symbolical language, for we have no
experience of any world but this, and
consequently no human words properly
to express either the abode and state of
the dead or the abode of God. And the
same applies to all statements about the
being of God, except so far as He has
appeared as man in human experience;
and to much of the language used about
angels and about the creation of the world
and the last things. Of all matters which
lie outside human experience we can only
use symbolical or analogical language.
"We see through a glass darkly"—an

enigmatic reflection as in a metal mirror.
The mercy is that in Christ God has so
manifested Himself within human experience that we can speak of Him also in the
language of literal historical facts. That
is the glory of our creed.

The redemptive work of our Lord is
manifold, but it may be summarized under
three heads. It is example, atonement,
new life—or the pattern set *before us*, the
sacrifice offered *for us*, the new life
wrought *in us*.

1. *The example or pattern of human life.*
By His words He has taught us all that
human life may be, when lived in the light
of God. By His deeds He showed what
power can work in human life to dispel
disease and misery. By all His conduct
He proved how rich and glorious a thing
human life can be. Henceforth the world
can never forget it. Cynics and pessimists
stand for ever rebuked. There is the true
Son of Man. The fruit of constant meditation on the Gospels is to fix in our souls
indelibly an image which will never suffer
us to be content in ourselves or others
with sensuality or selfishness or bitterness
or contempt or hypocrisy or worldliness.

2. *Atonement.* But what of the past,
the horrible, ever self-renewing past of
humanity and of myself? How can we

escape the contagion of the world and of our own selves? How can we break the chain and sequence of sin? All the world over men have been seeking God and coming before Him with offerings and sacrifices, feeling that God must have of their best, and seeking to render themselves acceptable to Him. But the conclusion is ever the same—that God does not want those things, for they are His own already; and "the blood of bulls and of goats cannot take away sin." Meanwhile the man himself remains conscious in his innermost soul that he cannot break with his own past or the past of humanity to which he belongs: "I am a man of unclean lips, and I dwell among a people of unclean lips." It is to this sort of feeling that the preaching of the atonement has appealed. And there is no doubt how universal its appeal has been.

In Jesus Christ our manhood took a fresh start. He is true man, but new man—wholly free from the taint of sin. He alone realizes perfectly the guilt of sin, because He alone does not share it. He alone realizes perfectly what man ought to be towards God. His life from end to end is a perfect sacrifice. When the sin which is in the world refused Him and rejected Him, because men would not

part from their selfishness, their indolence,
and their pride—when sin in the people of
Israel closed in upon Him and brought
Him to the cross—He recognized in the
cross the will of God, and was obedient
unto death.   There at last in blood and
agony He accomplished His sacrifice of
perfect obedience.   This is the New Man's
act of reparation for all the lawlessness and
wilfulness of the old humanity.   He offers
Himself without spot to God, and the perfect sacrifice of self is perfectly acceptable
to God.   It frees the hand of God to give
to man, in Him, all that He would give.
This is why the atonement is called also
propitiation.   Not because it changes the
disposition of God towards us, but because
it enables Him freely to exhibit His
mercy.

In Him mankind is reconciled to God.
He stands in will and intention for every
man, as on earth He identified Himself
with every man and disowned no one.
Actually it means that every one who will
come with entire faith in Him and become
by baptism identified with Him, however
sinful or imperfect he may be, can claim
the forgiveness of his sins in His name,
and can make a fresh start from a new
standing-ground—in Christ.   He is washed
white in the blood of the Lamb.   This is

the doctrine of "Christ for us." There are no sins too many or too great for God to forgive. There is no one who cannot break with his past and start afresh. Wholly without reference to any merits of ours, simply by the free gift of God's unmerited love, we can, every one of us, identify ourselves with Christ by faith, and that a thousand times over after a thousand relapses, and in His name be reconciled to God—absolved and set free from all the guilt of the past : " I will run the way of Thy commandments, because Thou hast set my heart at liberty."

3. But it is quite plain that the redemption of man must be something within him. If he is alienated from God nothing can restore him except such inward restoration as makes him once again Godlike. There is no fellowship with God possible except in likeness to God. This is the central and continuous witness of the Bible. Thus no view of our redemption by Christ would be tolerable which should find its sole or its chief expression in anything done *for us*. That can only be the prelude to what is done *in us*. The moral difficulties which have been felt so widely about the Christian doctrine of the atonement have been due in part to this consideration being ignored. Christ for

us has been separated from Christ in us.
But this is quite unjustifiable. Our Lord
is represented in the Gospels as plainly
instructing His disciples that their future
enlightenment and inward renewal by
His Spirit would be something far greater
than anything which He could do for
them while He was among them. Moreover, substitution is a very poor word to
describe our Lord's relation to us even
in His sacrifice.

He always appears as claiming men's
identification with Himself in the spirit
of His sacrifice. No idea of forgiveness
which is consistent with a refusal on our
own part of service and sacrifice can, for
a moment, be read into Christ's words or
those of His apostles. But His identification with men was very imperfect while
He was still among them as one among
many. Accordingly His glorification in
heaven is represented as only the necessary beginning of His full activity among
men. If the heavens cleaved around His
ascending form and hid it from sight, it is
but a few days before they cleave again
around the descending Spirit; and that
Spirit comes not so much to supply His
absence as to accomplish His presence,
His presence with men in His body, which
is the church.

THE HOLY SPIRIT

Spirit means breath or life. Thus the Spirit of God is that person of the ever-blessed Trinity who represents the breath or life of God. Thus "the Spirit of the Lord filleth the world." All the life of nature and all the activities of man, social, industrial, and artistic, are in the Old Testament ascribed to the Spirit. But because God's righteous character is the attribute of God which is there most emphasized, so the Spirit is before all else Holy Spirit, and He cannot dwell with unrighteousness and sin.

Only here and there a man, prophet or other, is recognized as possessed of the Holy Spirit. But a more abundant outpouring is anticipated not only upon the Christ who is to be, but also upon His people, universally, in the day of Christ. And it is this anticipation which is fulfilled through Jesus Christ, so fully that by comparison the Holy Spirit is spoken of as given for the first time in the great outpouring on the Day of Pentecost. Thus the distinguishing marks of the Pentecostal outpouring are two.

1. The Holy Spirit came down from the uplifted Christ, the head of the new and redeemed humanity, to fill the company and

fellowship of men who are to carry on His work in the world; so that they shall be His organ or "body," in which He can live, and through which He can act, by His Spirit which He has given them.

2. The other distinguishing mark of this new gift of the Spirit is that it is freely given to all the members of the body. They are already, and are to continue to be, a body with different functions. There are apostles and other members, men and women. But on all alike is the Holy Spirit poured out for enlightenment and for strength, for work and for witness. And if an early Christian had been asked what, as distinguished from other men, a Christian is, he would have given one of two answers—either that he is a man who has come to believe in Jesus as Christ and Lord, or that he is a man who has, and knows he has, received His Spirit. But I must say more about this when I come, very soon, to write about the ministry of the Spirit.

THE HOLY TRINITY

Now we must pause for a moment reverently to consider the effect of all this redemptive work of God for men upon their thought of God. The name of God

—the Jehovah or Lord of the Old Testament—has become to them now the name of the Father, about whom Jesus Christ had taught them so abundantly as His Father and theirs; and the name of the Son, Jesus Christ Himself, who had come out of the bosom of the Father to reveal Him, in whom they believed and whom they worshipped; and the name of the Spirit — the Holy Spirit through whom they had abiding union with the Son and the Father.

The name of God is henceforth the name of the Father and of the Son and of the Holy Ghost, three persons—so they came to express it, using the best word they could find—in one God. For "the Father is God and the Son is God and the Holy Ghost is God, and yet they are not three Gods, but one God." "In this Trinity there is no before or after, no greater or less, but the whole three persons are coeternal together and co-equal"—Trinity in Unity and Unity in Trinity.

This formula was the outcome of the original experience of the church. At the side of the eternal Father was a Son, whom as man among men they had come to know, whom they had come to believe in as very God of very God; and from

the Father and the Son had come forth
the Spirit whom Christ had spoken of
as "another," whom they had learned to
think of as a living, divine person with
whom they had to deal.   And these
divine three they knew were not three
Gods.   It was but the one God of
Israel's old faith more fully disclosing
Himself.   The three moreover are not
separable individuals. ✓ Wherever the
Father acts, He acts through the Son,
whether in creation or redemption, and
by His Spirit.   Wherever the Son acts,
it is the Father who is acting in Him;
and when He sends the Spirit, the Spirit
in His coming brings the Son and the
Father.   It is one only God.   Only as
God has come nearer to men to redeem
them something of His inner being has
been disclosed.   It is not a monotonous
unity that reveals itself, but an eternal
fellowship of Father, Son, and Spirit.
That is to say, it is the sort of unity
which we can think of as alive and real,
even before ever the world was.   In
the mutual relationship of the divine
persons we can understand how God in
His eternal being is Love; and we can
understand further why when He calls
men unto fellowship with Himself it is
always in society and not as isolated

individuals: it is as a family, or a nation or a church; in any case as a fellowship of some sort. Because God Himself is eternal fellowship and eternal love, loneliness and selfishness cannot express Him.

HUMAN NATURE AND SIN. ANGELS AND DEVILS

It is sometimes remarked that there is very little about man or sin in the Creeds, except just at the end. This is because it is the main purpose of the Creeds to summarize what God has done for man, and revealed about Himself in doing it. But there is much about man that is taken for granted; otherwise men could not have been the subjects of divine redemption, nor could the Lord of all have been made man.

What is taken for granted is that man was made "in God's image"—that is to say, that he is spirit as well as body, a personality and not a thing, endowed with intelligence and free-will, and made to be God's vicegerent in the world which was entrusted to his government. It is the sense of this great dignity of man which is renewed in our minds as we contemplate the Son of Man. And the motive of the divine redemption lies in the fact that our race, though created for so lofty a vocation, has plunged so deep into sin and has so deeply defaced in themselves the image of God, that only the self-sacrificing act of God in redeeming them can raise them from ruin or enable them to realize the purpose of God. "Neither is there any other name under heaven, that is given among men, save the name of Jesus, wherein we must be saved."

It is possible for one who thinks only of God's majesty to despise men. The over-whelming thought of the sovereignty of God in the mind of some of the greatest Christians, S. Augustine and Calvin [1] for instance, has made them disparage or ignore man's right to be equitably treated.

But God has in fact given men such a right in making them persons and giving them a conscience. And the doctrine of the Bible as a whole, and of our Lord in particular, recognizes to the full the dignity bestowed upon every single child of man by his Creator, and the equitable and more than equitable love of God for each and every one—" who will have all men to be saved and to come to the knowledge of the

[1] I do not think that S. Paul can justly be accused of this.

truth "—" who is the saviour of all men,"
if they will only have it so.

And the Bible has a profoundly simple
explanation of the terrible condition of
humanity, which seems to cry out against
the very idea either of man's dignity or
of God's justice. The explanation is sin.
The disorder of the world is due to sin.
Voluntary correspondence with God is
only possible if refusal of correspondence
is also possible—that is lawlessness. This
is the Bible doctrine of sin. Sin is lawlessness. It is refusal to obey the will
of God: and there is not in the whole
universe any other kind of lawlessness.
It is the foolish claim of the creature to
be independent of the Creator that has
wrought all this havoc. That is why man
needs to be redeemed.

And we must extend our view beyond
the bounds of mankind. In this vast universe there is no reason to suppose that
men are the only free and intelligent
beings. Indeed it is almost unimaginable.
Certainly our Lord and the prophets and
apostles would have us believe that beyond man there are vast hosts of intelligent
spirits, good and bad, angels and devils.
And the struggle between good and evil
in this world is thus thrown upon the
background of a vaster scene of conflict.

" We wrestle not against flesh and blood,
but against the principalities, against the
powers, against the world-rulers of this
darkness, the spiritual hosts of wicked-
ness." "Your adversary the devil, as a
roaring lion, walketh about, seeking whom
he may devour : whom withstand steadfast in your faith." [1]   And the good angels
are not only the worshipping host of
heaven, not only mysterious forces in
nature, but also "ministering spirits sent
forth to do service" for men.

But into this dimly-known background
of human life we must carry back the
same principle. All created beings were
made by God in love and for good. If
they have become evil, it is because they
have used against God, by a perverted
freedom, the power that was given them
to use for Him. Wherever sin is, it is
lawlessness.

And it does not need any revelation,
either in any other age or to-day, to tell
us how deep and wide is the havoc which
sin has wrought. All men have sinned.
And sin has been disastrous in its effects,
as is shown in experience. And because
men are not entirely individual, but are
united by physical and social bonds in
families and races and the one common

[1] Eph. vi. 12; 1 S. Pet. v. 8.

race, so sin has infected and disordered
the whole race of mankind. It is already
in us before the beginning of our personal
consciousness. "In sin hath my mother
conceived me." This is the Christian
doctrine of sin, "actual" and "original,"
or individual and social.

No student of this doctrine, in particular
no student of the teaching of Jesus Christ,
will ever echo the foolish idea that sin is
a survival in us of our animal ancestry
which we are outgrowing. True it infects
the body; but its seed is in the spirit. It
is wilfulness and selfishness—the refusal of
God. Our Lord will not let us think that
bodily sins — drunkenness and lust — are
worse than selfishness and pride, or that the
sin of the barbarian is any way greater or
more serious than the sin of the highly civil-
ized man. In fact the opposite is the case.
Sin accompanies every stage of human
development, and threatens with disaster
every individual and every civilization.
And such is the respect with which God
treats the freedom of man that He endures
all the awful havoc which sin has made,
while everywhere, in the soul of every
human being, and on the great stage of
the world, He is working for redemption
—redemption which is by sacrifice.

That is the call of Christ, then—the call

to redemption. There is no one who does not need to be redeemed. It is true that Christ does more than redeem us — He brings us to perfection. Man was created at the bottom of the ladder of progress. He was not created perfect, but only capable of attaining perfection by the grace of God. The humanity which is revealed in Christ is not humanity as it was created, but humanity at the very height of its possibilities. Christ consummates humanity as well as redeems it. None the less, every single human being is in sin, and needs redemption, and not merely development. He needs a fresh start—to be converted or turned; to be regenerated or grafted upon a fresh stock —the stock of Christ.

But this, and the great and eternal destiny of man, we shall have to consider in succeeding chapters.

CHAPTER IV

The Church and the Sacraments

WHEN the Holy Spirit came down from Christ in heaven on the day of Pentecost, He came to fill with Christ's own life the church which had been already gathered to await His coming. Henceforth the church is Christ's body, one organism (if I may so speak) with its Head in heaven,[1] and His living instrument for His work in the world. Thus it stands a visible institution in history from the first chapter of the Acts of the Apostles onward, awaiting the conversion of individuals to Christ. The individual converts did not combine to form the church. It was there before them. Conversion leads necessarily to incorporation in the church. It could lead to nothing else: for there is no belonging to Christ

---

[1] S. John, we should note, represents our Lord as speaking of Himself as " the vine " of which we men are the branches—branches included in the vine ; and S. Paul speaks similarly of Christ as consisting of the Head and the members.   See S. John xv. 5, 1 Cor. xii. 12.

39

except by membership in His body. As the Gospel is preached in city after city churches arise—the church of Corinth, the church of Ephesus, and so on; but each of these churches is the local representative of the one church. It is all one gradually expanding fellowship: the church is one as Christ is one: holy because consecrated in Him by His Spirit: catholic because there can be in it "neither Jew nor Greek, male nor female, barbarian, Scythian, bond nor free." It is the destined home of all human beings simply in virtue of their being men or women. It is one all-embracing community, destined to extend itself to the ends of the earth, and bind in one faith and fellowship all kinds and classes of men.

The idea that the essence of Christianity lies in a merely individual faith in Christ, and that church membership is a secondary thing, is not to be found in the New Testament. The fatherhood of God and the salvation wrought by Christ are to be realized only in the brotherhood of men, which is the church. It is very difficult for men, different as they are in temperament, class, and race, to become or to remain one brotherhood. The New Testament abundantly illustrates the difficulty. In overcoming it is to be found the real triumph of Christ. "He hath made both (Jew and Gentile) one." According to the New Testament all men by their true nature are intended for brotherhood, but only in Christ can they really become brothers. Thus, the church is "the brotherhood." S. Paul would not have tolerated for a moment the idea of two churches at Corinth or Ephesus, one for Jews and one for Gentiles, or one for free men and one for slaves. He would not have tolerated the idea that a man can first believe and then choose which church to belong to. There can be only one church to which all believers are, by their faith, bound to belong. It is Christ who by His sacrifice has broken down the barriers between man and man, and made it possible for men in Him to accomplish the difficult task of realizing and maintaining unity.

But we must stop to consider two difficulties which naturally present themselves to our minds.

1. The doctrine of "salvation only in the church" seems a narrow doctrine from two points of view—first, because it has been interpreted to mean that everlasting misery is the destiny of all who are not members of the church, whether

heathen abroad or unbelievers at home.
But this is a mistake. We know for
certain the character of God as it is revealed in Jesus Christ. We know that
in a real sense all men by their very
nature belong to Christ in whom "all
things," and much more all rational beings,
"consist." We know also that God's
opportunities extend beyond the limits of
this life. He will deal equitably with
every soul. He alone can judge. He will
never condemn any one who has tried
honestly to be true to the best light he
had: of that we may feel quite sure. But
the great salvation which Christ brings is
to be a visibly manifested thing, as Christ
was visibly manifested. It is represented
by "a city set on a hill." It is a great
organized society going out into all the
world in the saving power of Christ.
When we say that salvation is to be found
only in the church we mean not something reserved in the unknown depths of
God's mercy, but something here and
now covenanted, accepted, experienced
and proclaimed.

2. But Christianity has been a long time
in the world, and there are all kinds of
Christian churches not in communion
with one another. It is surely narrow to
proclaim that there is only one church;

for, whatever definition you may give of
the church, you are sure to "unchurch"
a number of very excellent Christians who
belong to other communions which you
do not recognize. This is the greatest of
difficulties, and we must come back to it
before we have done. But now I would
ask you simply to consider, with a quiet
and determined contemplation, what is
the intention expressed in the New Testament, which is indeed the intention of
Christ. He meant all His disciples to be
one in a visible unity. There is no mention of any invisible church in this world.
And to-day, amid the clamour of our
class divisions, amid the horror of nomin-
ally Christian nations engaged in slaughter-
ing one another, we turn again longingly
to Christ's intention. It is schism that is
narrow, not catholicity. It is schism—providing a separate church for each nation,
a separate church for each class or each
distinctive disposition of men—it is schism
that makes the witness of Christ so feeble
in the world. And the doctrine of the one
catholic church, constraining all men
who profess belief in Christ to discipline
themselves enough to live in unbroken
fellowship—a fellowship which transcends
all natural divisions of race and class—it is
this alone that can give us a really broad

Christianity. "We are all one manhood in Christ Jesus." And, indeed, the world to-day would be far better off, the witness to Christ would be far better borne, if in every country we had but half the number that we now have of nominal Christians, but these maintaining the unity of the spirit in the bond of peace.

Our Lord, then, certainly meant all the believers in His name to feel the obligation of belonging to the one church. That is the unmistakable witness of the New Testament. The very difficulty of maintaining such a unity among all the differences of human nature is to be one main trial of the sincerity of our faith. And the reality of our obligation to maintain the unity of the society is brought home to us by the institution of visible sacraments as instruments of spiritual grace.

THE SACRAMENTS

The sacraments are "outward and visible signs of an inward and spiritual grace given unto us." In their principle they are in harmony with the whole system of the material universe. For everything visible in the world expresses some spiritual meaning and contains some spiritual force. We men ourselves are embodied spirits, and spiritual reality must come home to us, like all other reality, through our bodily organs. It is in accordance with the deep necessity of our being that "The Word was made flesh, and dwelt among us." And the church with its visible sacraments is the extension in idea and in reality of the incarnation. The gifts of God in Christ are not to depend upon our subjective feelings, but upon the will of God, and are guaranteed to our wills by the outward sign.

But also the sacraments are social ceremonies—ceremonies connected with membership. Baptism, as taken over by the catholic from the Jewish church, was regarded not only as a ceremony of personal cleansing, but also as admission into the holy community. "By one Spirit were we all baptized into one body." Confirmation is an outward blessing of each admitted member by the local head of the community, and conveys to him his equipment for full membership. The Holy Communion is a common sharing of the one bread and the one cup—the speaking symbols of membership. Absolution is restoration to the fellowship of the community, Ordination is appointment to office in the community. Thus, by making

sacraments, visible ceremonies of a visible
society, to be the instruments of spiritual
grace to the individual—by making these
social sacraments to be the provided
means of personal salvation—God has
made it apparent that His salvation is
no gift to isolated individuals, but a gift
given to members of a body, a gift for
membership.

Only it needs to be remembered that
when we say that the great sacraments
are "generally necessary to salvation" we
do not limit the power of God to give to
individuals what He wills to give, outside
all sacraments, in this life or beyond it.
We are speaking of salvation in the sense
explained above as something open, covenanted, and proclaimed.

As to the number of the sacraments
there has been much controversy. If you
take the general definition of sacraments
to be "outward and visible signs of an
inward and spiritual grace given" you
may reckon a large number of sacraments.
If you add to your definition "ordained
by Christ Himself"—that is, ordained by
Him in their outward form during His
earthly ministry as recorded in the four
Gospels, then you must reckon them as
two only. But, in accepting this definition,
the Church of England, in our present

Prayer Book, does not exclude the use of the word sacrament in a less restricted sense. I propose in this book to treat as sacraments, besides the two great "sacraments of the Gospel" *Baptism* and the *Holy Communion*, also *Confirmation*—which is the apostolic completion of baptism,—the reconciliation of the penitent or *Penance*, *Matrimony*, *Ordination*, and *Unction of the Sick*, which, in the greater part of the catholic church, are reckoned as the sacraments.[1]

I must add that sacraments were entrusted to the church, which has authority, under Christ, to "bind" and "loose," that is to legislate with divine sanction; and therefore, except so far as the outward ceremony was fixed once for all by the authority of Christ and His apostles, the church must be regarded as having authority to determine the conditions of administration—that is, to decide what constitutes a "valid" sacrament, meaning by the word "valid" a sacrament which the church recognizes and ratifies. A sacra-

[1] There is considerable ancient authority for speaking of only two sacraments if confirmation is included in baptism, or of three if confirmation is reckoned apart. But so much misunderstanding has resulted from not reckoning as sacraments matrimony, ordination and the reconciliation of penitents that I think we had better reform—not our doctrine but our nomenclature.

ment may be irregular in the conditions
of its administration, but still valid and
not to be repeated.   I hope I need not add
that God is not tied by conditions of
validity, but can give His blessing where
and how He sees fit.   But every society
must have for its official action conditions
of validity.

Before I go on further I would seek to
kindle the imagination of my readers with
a sense of the profound adaptation of the
whole system of church and sacraments to
the moral needs of men.   As fellowship
in a nation supports each citizen and
guarantees his freedom ; as fellowship in
a regiment sustains a soldier's courage
when, alone, he might fail ; as fellowship
in a trade-union supports the solitary
worker with the protection of comradeship
—so fellowship in the church is meant to
sustain the weakness of the individual,
through all experiences of failure and
disillusionment ; the sympathy of a common creed is meant to carry him through
periods of depression and vacillation ;
and the gifts of divine grace as embodied
and guaranteed in sacraments are meant
to lift him out of the vagaries of subjective emotion upon the solid ground cf
objective reality.

Now I propose to deal with the sacraments in detail, and because it is of their very essence to be definite ceremonies, I propose to state with regard to each what, in the common judgement of the church, is the outward part of the sacrament that is *the matter* or visible material and action, and *the form* or words defining the purpose and meaning of the sacrament; what *the inward spiritual grace*; of what sort is the appointed *minister*; and who are the *subjects* or proper recipients of the sacrament.

Holy Baptism.—Most respectable societies, existing for any permanent objects, have some ceremony of initiation or incorporation. Baptism, then, is the ceremony of incorporation into Christ and His church. Its outward *matter* is washing with water.[1] Its *form* is "I baptize thee[2] in the name of the-Father and of the Son and of the Holy Ghost." The priest is the proper *minister*, but baptism by any baptized individual is allowed, and every Christian should be ready to baptize in an emergency. Its *inward and spiritual grace*, that is, the gift which, by the will of God, is declared to accompany the ceremony, is incorporation into Christ. The baptized

---

[1] It should be at least a real *pouring* of water, and not merely a sprinkling.

[2] In the Eastern Church it is "N., the servant of God, is baptized in the name, etc."

H

person who has hitherto been only a member of our sinful humanity is hereby
regenerated by the Holy Ghost; that is,
he receives a new birth or incorporation
into Christ and His body. He becomes
a member of Christ's family, with all the
privileges of membership; and can claim,
in Christ's name, the forgiveness of his
sins. "We acknowledge one baptism for
the remission of sins." This is the plain
teaching of the New Testament and of the
Prayer Book.[1] I say that he can *claim*, in
Christ's name, the forgiveness of his sins:
for sacraments are not charms. They are
indeed in themselves effective instruments
of divine grace; but, because we are
rational beings, God can do nothing for us
without our co-operation. And baptism
will do a man no spiritual good unless he,
by faith, will claim as his own the gifts
which baptism has given him. Any unbaptized person may be the *subject* of
baptism.

The baptismal services of the church
were drawn up in the first instance for
adults capable in their own persons of
renouncing the life of sin from which
Christ redeems them, and professing their

[1] See S. John iii. 5; Acts ii. 38, xxii. 16; Rom. vi.
3; 1 Cor. xii. 13; Titus iii. 5: cf. the catechism and
the service of baptism.

belief in the Christian creed after due instruction, and their intention to obey and follow Christ. Solemn vows to this effect have always been required of those to be baptized. But, apparently from the first, the children of Christian parents have been admitted into church membership by baptism in their infancy, and spon-sors representing the church have an-swered on their behalf, and have guaran-teed their Christian education if they should survive infancy. Without some such guarantee the church does not au-thorize the baptism of infants. Indis-criminate baptism of infants is simply an abuse.

Confirmation, or the laying on of hands.— From the beginning the laying on of hands by the apostles followed baptism. Thus baptism and the laying on of hands taken together (and sometimes called by the one name of baptism) were held in the early church to constitute the ceremony of initiation into the Christian society. And both together were solemnly administered only at the season of Easter each year. But the bishop's presence being needed for the second part of the ceremony, and not for the first, the desire not to defer baptism has led to the separation in the Western Church of the two parts—of

confirmation from baptism.   Nevertheless they should still be regarded as the
two parts of the one ceremony, and it is
intended that both should be publicly
administered.   The proper *matter* of
confirmation is the laying on of hands
(to which in early days unction with oil
was added, but it is not necessary).   The
proper *form* is some formula of blessing
which makes mention of or implies the
gift of the Holy Ghost.   The *inward and
spiritual grace* is the gift of the Holy Ghost
to strengthen the person confirmed, and
to equip him or her for membership.[1]
For, as in ordination, the laying on of
hands symbolizes consecration for service,
and the confirmed person should be taught
to regard himself as a fully-equipped member of Christ, that is equipped for service
and endowed with all the duties and rights
of membership, and as sharing the kingship and priesthood of the whole body of
Christ.   The *minister* of confirmation is
the bishop.[2]   The *subject* of confirmation
is any baptized person.   In England, confirmation being reserved to the years of

[1] See Acts viii. 17, 18 ; xix. 6.
[2] This is so quite exclusively in the Anglican Communion ; in the Roman Church with very slight
exception ; in the Eastern Church only indirectly
so, in that the bishop blesses the oil which is the
instrument of confirmation.

discretion, that is, the time when the child can understand and learn and choose for himself, and baptism being generally administered in infancy, the person to be confirmed is required before his confirmation to renew the promises of his baptism. The age of confirmation has been the subject of much discussion, but certainly the Prayer Book suggests an earlier age than has of recent years been customary among us.

The Holy Communion.—The greatest of all the sacraments of the church is the Holy Communion—the greatest because it sums up in itself such an incomparable richness of spiritual meaning and force; because of the glory of the presence and gift there vouchsafed; because it perpetuates both Bethlehem and Calvary; because it evokes all the powers and faculties of the worshipping soul; because it is commended to us as the Lord's own service—"This do in remembrance of me." As we read the four accounts of its institution,[1] its elementary meaning becomes plainly intelligible. At the Last Supper with His disciples, Jesus took bread and blessed it, and brake, and gave it to them saying, "Take, eat, this is my body," and they

[1] S. Matt. xxvi. 26 ff.; S. Mark xiv. 22 ff.; S. Luke xxii. 19 ff.; 1 Cor. xi. 23 ff.

all partook of the one bread. And He
took the cup and blessed it, and gave it
to them saying, "Drink ye all of this, for
this is my blood of the new covenant
which is poured out for you for the remission of sins." And they all drank of
the one cup. This simple ceremony speaks
for itself. It means sharing together; and
that in which they are to share together
is He Himself, whose body was broken
and whose blood was shed to redeem
them. When our Lord said, "Do this
in remembrance of me," and so made this
speaking ceremony the central sacrament
of His religion, He must have meant that
the communion (or sharing together) of
all His people in Him, who died for
them, was to be its governing idea. But
we must examine the rite a little more
closely to take in its meaning in different
aspects.

1. It is the communication of Christ
to each receiver. The priest, the officer
of the church, repeating what Christ
our Lord did and said when He instituted
these holy mysteries, consecrates the
bread to be His body and the wine to
be His blood, that we receiving these
outward things may feed on Christ, may
eat His flesh and drink His blood. We
cannot analyse the mystery. Christ is

made present there in His body and in
His blood under the humble form of
bread and wine. While with our eyes
we see nothing but the outward gifts,
by faith we behold heavenly things made
present amongst us. True, in the bread
broken and the wine outpoured, separate
the one from the other, we see the
remembrance of a transaction upon this
earth, the sacrifice of Calvary. But if
we inquire into the spiritual reality, we
know that it is not the dying Christ but
the living Christ—Christ as He is in the
heavenly places—who is here to feed us
with His own life under these humble
forms. "Christ herein imparteth Himself, even His whole entire person, to
every soul that receiveth Him." He who
was our example outwardly is now by His
Spirit given to be our new and inward
life, to dwell continually in our hearts,
and to renew us into His own likeness,
strengthening our weakness, and purify-
ing our uncleanness. And in the whole
process of the sacrament we recognize
the characteristic work of the Holy Spirit,
who in the consecration brings the presence
of Christ, who Himself communicates Him
to the receiver.

2. But it is not merely a gift to the individual receiver; it is a sharing together

or communion in the body and blood of
Christ. We share together, not merely
with those who are kneeling at the same
altar, but with all Christ's people, the
living and the dead, the great company
which no man can number, in one communion and fellowship. Thus the body
of Christ renews the body which is His
church, and the blood, which is the life
of Christ, reinvigorates its common life.
We need, more than can easily be said,
to recall to the consciousness of each
communicant that his every communion
lays upon him the privilege and the
obligation of behaving as a brother to
every other communicant, "girding himself with humility to serve them." We
have very few communicants amongst us
compared to what we ought to have; but
it would be a different England if every
one of them behaved as if he really
believed S. Paul's words [1]—"The cup of
blessing which we bless, is it not a communion in the blood of Christ? The
bread which we break, is it not a communion in the body of Christ? Seeing
that we, who are many, are one bread,
one body; for we all partake of the one
bread."

3. Finally, the eucharist (as it is called)

[1] 1 Cor. x. 16, 17.

is the great Christian sacrifice. According to the doctrine of the Bible the only sacrifice acceptable to God is a spiritual sacrifice: that means the sacrifice of a person, and of words or things only as the expressions of a person. In the holy eucharist we come solemnly before God, as His people met for the commemoration of our redemption, to present to Him the sacrifice of our persons and our goods, our alms and our oblations, our prayers and our praises. And it is our own symbolic gifts of bread and wine that are consecrated to become the body and the blood of our Redeemer, the body that was broken and the blood that was shed for us. Thus, by His presence among us, all our imperfect and sin-stained sacrifices are brought into union with Christ's one full, perfect, and sufficient sacrifice, which was once offered for us, but is ever pleaded in the heavenly places. Thus in every eucharist the one perfect sacrifice is pleaded amongst us afresh. And, when we have fed upon Him, we ourselves are joined to His sacrifice; and in Him we offer ourselves, our souls and bodies to be all together a reasonable, holy, and lively sacrifice unto God who made us. This is indeed the end of our being.

In this way we may strive imperfectly

to summarize and express, what still remains inexpressible, the meaning of this august mystery. Here is the whole Christian truth in its every aspect. Here is the whole Blessed Trinity at work: here is the incarnation and the atonement perpetuated and applied ; here is union with the heavenly Christ, and the eager expectation of His second coming—" Ye do show the Lord's death till He come ; " here is the stimulus alike to divine worship and to human brotherhood ; here is the satisfaction of the innermost longing of the heart of man for union with God.

It is a terrible mistake to have allowed the Lord's service to become anything else than the central service of the morn-ing of the Lord's Day. As things are the vast majority of the members of the church never receive the blessed sacrament : millions of the baptized never join in the only divinely-appointed act of Christian worship—the most easily intel-ligible, because the most dramatic, of all services—and indeed are barely conscious of what is there enacted.

I know what is the obstacle to restoring the Lord's service to its proper place. It is the strength of the tradition which puts the chief service at eleven o'clock. Now that we have become more widely desirous to obey·the rule of the ancient church, that the body of Christ should be the first food that passes our lips, the eucharist celebrated with music and a sermon at eleven o'clock as the chief service of the Sunday is apt to become a celebration with very few communicants, or none at all except the priest. And, in spite of the example of the Roman and Eastern churches, in their later course, a great many of us, even of those who have no prejudice whatever against the attendance at the service of the altar of those who are not communicating, feel that the chief service should be the corporate communion, the service at which the most communicate, as it was in the catholic church everywhere for wellnigh the first thousand years of its life. I am convinced that we cannot habitually separate the offering of the sacrifice from the act of communion without grave loss. I cannot help looking longingly, and not without hope, for a state of things when the chief service of the Sunday shall be at an hour when all can communicate who are qualified and prepared.

Before we leave this great theme it ought to be said that the *matter* of this holy sacrament is bread, leavened or unleavened, and wine or wine mingled

with a little water; and the *form* the
act and words of consecration; and the
minister a priest; and the *subjects* (or proper
recipients) all baptized and confirmed
persons (or such as at least are ready and
willing to be confirmed) who have not
subsequently been put out of communion,
but can approach the holy sacrament in
faith and repentance.

Reconciliation of Penitents, or Penance.—
Sin is not only a private matter between
the soul and God; it is a weakening of the
whole life of the church—however secret
it may be. The church is wronged by
any and every sin. It is this feeling in
part, I suppose, which causes S. James
to exhort Christians thus—"Confess your
sins one to another, and pray one for
another, that ye may be healed."[1]   It is
also certain that Christians from the
beginning believed that our Lord had left
to His church the power to absolve or
retain sins. S. John records His solemn
grant of this power to the eleven on the
day on which He rose from the dead.
"Receive ye the Holy Ghost: whosesoever
sins ye forgive, they are forgiven unto
them; and whosesoever sins ye retain, they
are retained."[2]   Whatever other application these words may have, at least one

[1] S. Jas. v. 16.   [2] S. John xx. 22, 23.

principal application was to members of
the church who fell into scandalous sin.
Such persons were put out of communion
and, when they had shown marks of
true penitence or "done penance," were
readmitted to communion in some formal
way, as by prayer and the laying on of
hands of the bishop. This was done, as
S. Paul says,[1] "in the person of Christ,"
the action of the church being regarded
as the action of Christ Himself in the
church. That is the essence of the
church doctrine of "penance"—the duty
of the church to judge its members, and
the authority of the church to retain or
forgive their sins. And this is a properly
sacramental action, because the formal
action of the church in absolving or
reconciling penitents carried with it the
action of Christ. This system of penance
was applied in the first instance, as I have
said, to sins which caused scandal, to open
sins. In the Church of England at the
Reformation it was desired to restore,
as far as possible, this system of public
penance; and one of the Thirty-Nine
Articles (the thirty-third) speaks of such
notorious sinners as being excommunicated
and then "openly reconciled by penance."
In our old parish books there are frequent

[1] 2 Cor. ii. 10.

notices of such public penances down into
the eighteenth century.

But besides this, from the beginnings of
the church its members are found volun-
tarily confessing their secret sins—at first
in the public congregation, later to the
bishop or priest appointed to receive such
confessions ; and then doing penance and
being absolved, at first publicly and then
privately. In the Middle Ages such private
or auricular confession of all grave or
mortal sins was made obligatory, which
it had not been in earlier times. At the
Reformation all such obligation was re-
moved, and the matter now stands with us
thus. The authority of the priesthood to
absolve is strongly maintained.   The
words of the ordination of a priest among
us run thus : " Receive the Holy Ghost
for the office and work of a priest in the
church of God here committed unto thee
by the imposition of our (the bishop's)
hands : whose sins thou dost forgive they
are forgiven, and whose sins thou dost
retain they are retained," etc. And the
following form of absolution is (in the
Order for the Visitation of the Sick)
given to the priest to use : " Our Lord
Jesus Christ, who hath left power to His
church to absolve all sinners who truly
repent and believe in Him, of His great

mercy forgive thee thine offences ; and by His authority committed to me, I absolve thee from all thy sins, in the name of the Father and of the Son and of the Holy Ghost." As in the ancient church, it is strongly maintained in our Prayer Book, that all worthy penitence, without any sacramental confession or absolution, is met by the fullest forgiveness of God. But any one who cannot quiet his own conscience, but requires further comfort or advice, is exhorted to come to the parish priest, "or to some other discreet and learned minister of God's word, and open his grief ; that by the ministry of God's holy word he may receive the benefit of absolution, together with ghostly counsel and advice, to the quieting of his conscience and avoiding of all scruple and doubtfulness." Besides this, on their sick-beds people are to be "moved" to confess their sins to the priest, if they feel their conscience "troubled with any weighty matter."

Circumstances have changed greatly since the Reformation. Public penance has become more and more and more difficult to administer. The sense of sin has fallen in most men to a very low level. It is necessary for a living church to give directions suited to present-day needs.

All that I am at present authorized by
the church to say is that (where public
notorious sin is not in question) no priest
is justified in requiring any one to make
his confession ; and no priest is justified
in refusing the ministry of confession and
absolution to any penitent who desires it.
There has been of late years an immense
increase in the number of confessions
made : but if the gravity of sin was more
widely felt, I believe that multitudes more
would desire to submit themselves to the
judgement of the church through its ministers, seeing that the authority to judge
and to absolve has been so explicitly and
solemnly given it by Christ.

Of course, the ministers of the church
may exercise judgement wrongly just as
the preacher may misrepresent the divine
message.   Over all their mistaken judgements we must believe in the rectifying
action of God.   Still the fact remains that
to bind us to His church Christ deliberately
committed this tremendous authority to
fallible men.

The *outward sign* of absolution is some
formula or prayer of absolution spoken
after the confession of the penitent has
been made, and any necessary require-
ments, necessary as evidence of real
repentance, have been accepted : the *in-*

ward and spiritual grace is divine absolution
and the removal of the barriers to Communion : the *minister* is a priest : and the
subject is any baptized Christian who has
sinned and repented.

Holy Matrimony.—The religion of Christ
centres in the home as much as in the
church. And the sacredness of the home
is based upon holy matrimony—the life-
long union of man and woman. By civil
law marriage is required to be before an
appointed officer, minister of religion or
civil officer; and our ecclesiastical law requires the ministration of the priest. But
its essence lies in the deliberate contract
of the man and woman with one another.
It is sacramental only because ratified and
rendered indissoluble by God — "Those
whom God hath joined together let no
man put asunder." By our church law in
England a marriage, duly made and consummated, is strictly indissoluble except
by death ; and, while it admits of separation *a mensa et thoro*, allows of no such
divorce as would free either party, during
the lifetime of the other, to marry again.
Of this there can be no question. It is
the opinion of the best scholars that this
indissolubility represents the intention of
Christ; so the church in general has
interpreted it; so the present writer be-

K

lieves.   But there exists, apparently, in
S. Matthew's Gospel the permission for
the husband of an adulterous wife to
divorce his wife and marry again.

This we must believe to be a declension
from the standard of our Lord.   But we
cannot deny that it is within the com-
petence of any national church to admit
a relaxation so authorized.   Those who
desire such relaxation of our law must
move for its formal adoption.   Meanwhile
our church law admits no exception.   It
upholds the strict standard of Christ, and
the standard of the church at its best.
And those who break in this important
matter the law of the society to which
they belong must expect to forfeit the
privileges of communion.   This law of
indissoluble marriage has proved, as the
first disciples anticipated, a very hard
standard to maintain.   All sorts of evasions
have been adopted, and it is possible that
nowadays it could not be strictly maintained as the law of civil society.   But I
believe that the church is doing the will
of Christ in maintaining the law of indissoluble marriage as the requirement of
its communion.

One other matter must also be mentioned.   The church has so believed in
the union of husband and wife as to treat

the relatives of either party as the relatives of the other—to treat "affinity" as equivalent to "consanguinity." More than that, the church has believed this principle to be divine. At the Reformation the legitimacy of Queen Elizabeth depended on the doctrine that no ecclesiastical authority could dispense from it. Our modern state has broken through this principle at one point by sanctioning marriage with a deceased wife's sister; but our part of the church retains the old principle, and refuses sanction.[1]

Unction of the Sick.—There ought to be no question that our Lord would have us regard sickness and disease as (at least for the most part) an invasion of the evil one which we ought to resist and repel. And as a part of sanitary science, side by side with the ministry of the physician, we ought to recognize spiritual influences for the healing of the body. There certainly is such a thing as faith-healing. And of this ministry S. James speaks thus: "Is any among you sick? let him call for the elders of the church; and let them pray over him, anointing him with oil in the name of the Lord. And the

[1] The terminology of matter and form, etc., do not admit of any satisfactory application in the case of matrimony.

prayer of faith shall save him that is sick.
And if he have committed sins, it shall be
forgiven him."[1]   In accordance with this
passage, the church has generally administered Unction of the Sick: and
though, unfortunately as some of us think,
its misuse led to its abandonment as an
authorized and sacramental ordinance at
the Reformation, it is being restored
among us, with the sanction of many
individual bishops, who are willing to
bless the oil for this purpose, when any
sick person claims what S. James so
plainly counsels.   Let us indeed pray
that its restoration may be accompanied
by the restoration all along the line
of the right attitude of the church
towards disease, as being not only an
infliction to be patiently borne, but an
aggression of evil to be resisted both by
science and by faith, and expelled both
from the society and the individual, as far
as possible.   The wise know well how far
that expulsion might go.

Holy Orders.—Bishops and priests, as
ministers of Christ, have been already
mentioned repeatedly.   Christ Himself
instituted a ministry in the persons of
His apostles, intended plainly to endure

---

[1] S. Jas. v. 14.

to the end ;[1] and the apostolate stands at the beginning of the Acts with an un-questioned authority. Thus the church did not appoint the ministry ; it was there to start with, as appointed by Christ. There were the Twelve and men of like authority, such as Barnabas and Saul, who exercised a general ministry and a general authority ; and when local churches arose, "presbyters" (also called "bishops") were ordained by the apostles in each church, with deacons and, perhaps, deaconesses. In the New Testament there are also other figures, such as prophets and evangelists and teachers, whose exact position is not easy to define. And in the earliest period when the church was undoubtedly expecting the advent of Christ immediately, there was naturally no thought for the future. But even before the end of the apostolic age, when the church felt compelled to contemplate a longer future, it threw itself on the principle of succession—that is, the prin-ciple that the ministry as instituted by Christ was intended to be perpetual down the ages; so that every minister, who could rightly claim to be such, in any grade of office, must have received ordination from those in the church before him who had

[1] S. Matt. xxviii. 20 ; S. Luke xii. 41 ff.

authority to ordain and who had in their
turn received it step by step from the
apostles. The history of the way in
which the ministry of the later church
emerged out of the apostolic ministry
cannot be exactly traced. But we must
insist that in this, as in all other matters
not precisely ordered by Christ, the
church has authority to bind and loose;
and with an extraordinary unanimity of
judgement — a unanimity which lasted
down to the sixteenth century—it was
held for certain that the three chief orders
of the ministry were bishops, presbyters,
and deacons: that of these the bishops
held in succession from the apostles the
full authority and ministry of the word
and sacraments, with sole authority to
ordain the other ministers; that priests
held a minor priestly authority, especially
authority to celebrate the holy eucharist
and to absolve and to preach; and that
the deacons held a ministry of assistance.

The democratic principle in the appointment to the ministry was very fully recognized in early times: the people, it was
commonly agreed, should appoint the
persons whom the bishops should ordain,
and should choose the bishops themselves.
But the act of ordination—the laying on
of hands with accompanying prayer or

formula — was regarded as sacramental, an outward and visible sign of an inward and spiritual grace thereby given. So it was regarded from the beginning, as S. Paul had spoken to S. Timothy of "the gift that was in him by the laying on of his (S. Paul's) hands."

It will be plain to any one that the principle of the succession in the ministry is even a necessary element in the idea of a visible church. If there is one church, one visible society, to which all who are Christ's must needs belong, it must be made manifest where that church is to be found.

Continuity of doctrine is a great thing; but it is not enough. There must also be continuity of persons. Otherwise any group of dissatisfied individuals might go off by themselves and still say "We are the church." The obligation to continue in communion with the bishop provided the necessary bond. The succession of bishops guaranteed the continuity of the church, and the communion of bishops with one another was intended to guar-antee the unbroken fellowship of the church.

What has been done in this chapter is to outline the doctrine of the one holy

catholic church, with its ministry and
sacraments, as it was believed and taught
with astonishing unanimity for more than
fifteen hundred years in Christendom,
and as it is still maintained in the Church
of England. That it is maintained under
difficulties and in the face of objections
we know; and some of these difficulties
and objections, as urged both from the
Roman Catholic and from the Protestant
side, I hope briefly to consider in a later
chapter.

Meanwhile, what I have tried to do is
to give Churchmen a sense of the way
in which the doctrines of the visible
church and of the sacraments and of
the ministry hold together as parts of one
whole, and how that whole is rooted in
the intention of Christ and in the very
idea of the incarnation.

CHAPTER V

The Last Things and the Communion of Saints

THE END OF THE WORLD

THE church looks forward to an "end of the world"—that is, an end of the present familiar order of things, which is to usher in the future state, "the world to come"—that is, the kingdom or reign of God, when all rebellion and evil has been utterly overcome and purged away, and God shall be all in all. There are passages in the New Testament in which the visible church is identified with the kingdom, and other passages in which they are distinguished. Thus, while we belong to the church, we are taught to work and pray that God's kingdom may come, implying that it is not here at present. Perhaps on the whole we may say that the kingdom is something larger than the visible church, but that both are of one piece: that the church represents the kingdom in the present world and by its

73   L

prayers and activities prepares the way for its future coming. Thus the church is to expect with the most profound desire the "day of God," when God is to come into His own in the whole universe of things, and the undisputed and universal reign of His Christ is to begin.

As I have already said, the end of the world, like the beginning of the world, is presented to us in forms and images which are symbolical. But they are symbolical of what is to be actually true. In fact, it follows inevitably from any real belief in God as the one only creator and sustainer of the world, that one day He must vindicate Himself in His whole creation. Thus whenever the prophets of God in the Old Testament or the New see any kingdom or empire or institution or individual flouting God in arrogance and pride, they anticipate with assurance for such an institution or person, if not repentance, then overthrow. That is God's day. And the prophets treat each particular overthrow of an insolent creature of God, which has used against God the powers which come from Him, as a specimen of the great final day of the Lord in the whole universe ; and they commonly describe it in terms of the final universal convulsion. We must recognize

that the prophets had an inspired and
assured insight into the principles of
God's government of the world, and
accordingly they foresee what must happen
in a particular case—for instance, that
Babylon or apostate Jerusalem or persecuting Rome must be overthrown.
Thus they utter real predictions, which
have been fulfilled. But they have no
general knowledge of future history given
to them. In their anticipations they constantly foreshorten the future and give
freedom to their imagination in describing
the details. This is characteristic of
Biblical "apocalypses" or unveilings of
the future. There is an element of true
and definite prediction and also a large
element of symbolical scenery. It is only
in a very restricted sense that prophecy
can be described as "history written
beforehand." And those, for instance,
who have tried to construct history beforehand out of the materials of S. John's
"Revelation" have proved in almost all
instances remarkably wrong.

The really important point is that the
prophets were inspired to assure the faithful
people of God that nothing should prevail
against God or His Christ, and that, in spite
of all seeming failures, the day of the Lord
and of His Christ was sure. Our Lord

Himself uses the apocalyptic method. He has a definite prediction to make—that is, the destruction of apostate Jerusalem. This He predicts as about to occur in the present generation, and His prediction was fulfilled. It occurred in what we call the ordinary course of history, and there does not appear to be anything specially miraculous about it. But, after the manner of ancient prophets, our Lord treats this overthrow as God's act of judgement on the city which had rejected not only the servants of God, but the Son Himself; and He throws this overthrow of the apostate city and temple upon the background of the end of the world and His own coming in glory, as the triumphant Christ, to judge the quick and the dead. His language is symbolical, like that of the prophets; and, like theirs, His vision of the end is quite independent of time. He told His disciples before His passion that even He Himself did not know "the day or hour"; and, after His resurrection, He told them that the times and the seasons were reserved in the Father's own power. Moreover, in His own discourses as recorded in the Gospels, we find our Lord frequently using language which suggests gradual development in the future, and perplexing delays, as well as language which anticipates the great day of final divine intervention as if it were imme-diately to be expected.

That the first Christians did in fact expect "the end" in their own lifetime does not admit of doubt. And the belief that it must soon come has characterized most religious revivals. To converted souls it has seemed inconceivable that God should any longer tolerate the in-solence of men. We may well believe that it would have come much more speedily than in fact it has, if the church had been faithful in maintaining its witness and extending it into the whole world, instead of falling back into a fatal acquiescence in things as they are. But our Lord had prepared the minds of His disciples to see the assurance of "the end" in His resurrection, and its actual realization (in a sense) in His ascension and the mission of the Spirit and the establishment of the church ; so that when in actual experience the fall of Jerusalem came and "the end was not yet," the mind of the church was not perplexed. Their attention was turned to the next adver-sary—the insolent, persecuting empire of Rome ; and, taught of John, the seer of "the Apocalypse," they waited for the judgement of God upon Rome. By the

time of the fall of Rome, however, the
church had got too much at home in the
world to be as zealous for the end as it
had been in its bright beginnings.

To-day there are not many of us, I fear,
who really and passionately desire the end
of the world and the consummation of the
kingdom. But it remains true always and
everywhere that every institution which
ignores or resists God—every civilization
which seeks to build itself up on a merely
secular basis or on a basis of self-interest,
individual or corporate—on pleasure, or
avarice, or pride—must be overthrown.
It remains true that we are led, both by
revelation and experience, to expect the
vindication of God not merely by a gradual
development of the world into perfection,
but by a cataclysm or series of cataclysms
in which the forces of evil are overthrown
and God manifestly triumphs over them.
On a universal and final scale this is to be
the end of the world. It may well be that
the final manifestation of divine victory
will follow upon a state of things in which
God has seemed to be utterly defeated all
the world over, just as the resurrection
of Christ followed upon the seeming total
failure of the cross. But the wise Christian is content to wait and see, while he
holds the confident faith that Christ reigns,

supreme and unquestionable, and will one
day come into His own in the whole scene
of creation.

HEAVEN

On the whole, the anticipations of the
New Testament do not lead us to transfer
the scene of the kingdom of God from
earth to some other sphere called heaven.
Rather it describes a "return" of Christ
from heaven to earth, and (so to speak)
a fusion of heaven with earth, or a new
heaven and a new earth wherein dwelleth
righteousness, the centre of the whole new
world being the New Jerusalem, the perfected fellowship of humanity, the city of
God. I am sure that we make a mistake
if we attempt to translate the symbols
of the end into literal anticipations of
history. But the matter of greatest importance is that it is this creation of God,
and the humanity which we now know,
that, purged and transformed, are to supply the material of the kingdom of God.
Whatever the catastrophe through which
the world must pass, whatever the purging
process of judgement, whatever the transformation of matter, it is this world that
is to become the kingdom of God. Thus
no labour will ever really be lost which
we spend here upon the preparation for

the kingdom. All faithful work done in Christ's name, however much it seem to fail, is really laid up in God's treasury, and its fruits will at last appear. It will become a stone in the New Jerusalem. "Blessed are the dead which die in the Lord from henceforth: yea, saith the Spirit, that they may rest from their labours; for their works follow with them."[1]

THE RESURRECTION OF THE DEAD

All this belief in the kingdom to come has involved a belief in a life beyond death. It became plain with the flash of inspiration to the soul of Isaiah that the dead Israelites, who had died without seeing the great deliverance, must be raised again to share in it. "Thy dead shall live; my dead bodies shall arise. Awake and sing, ye that dwell in the dust: for the earth shall cast forth the dead."[2] It is most interesting to see how the ancient people of Israel came to that belief in a future life which before our Lord's time we find prevailing amongst them, with the exception of the small and aristocratic section of the Sadducees. It was not through dealings with the dead. They originally shared with all their neighbours a background of belief in

[1] Rev. xiv. 13.   [2] Isa. xxvi. 19.

the pit of "sheol," where the spirits of the dead—pale shadows of their former selves —subsist drearily somewhere underground. But they were sternly debarred from any attempt to have intercourse with the dead. Their religion was to be a religion of the active, sunlit world ; they were to see God's reign here and now. And they did see it ; but only partly. It dawned upon their collective mind, and was confirmed to them by here a prophet and there a psalmist, (1) that if there be a God, almighty and righteous, there must be some larger sphere than that of this world—this "wild and irregular scene"—for God to realize and reveal Himself. This world cannot be the end ; (2) that the intimate spiritual relationship into which God admits His saints — Abraham and Isaac and Jacob, Moses and Samuel and David — cannot end with death. This intimacy must be continued in the beyond. By constant dwelling on these two lines of thought and expectation the Jews came to believe not merely in "the immortality of the soul," but in "the resurrection of the dead." Among the Greeks there was always the feeling that the body was something degrading—the prison-house of the soul and its pollution. They were con-tent to expect a survival of souls only.

M

But by a much healthier instinct, anticipat-
ing the future of a still remote science, the
Jews felt that the body is an essential part
of the man. They were healthily un-
ashamed of the body and the bodily functions. Thus, if they thought of a future
life, they wanted a complete life: they
wanted a better body perhaps than this
present flesh, but certainly a body—and
for each man his own body to match the
more perfect world in which he should
find himself. And it was this anticipation,
itself wrought into their minds by divine
inspiration, which was confirmed in our
Lord's teaching, and which received its
first realization in experience in His resurrection from the dead.

Any one who reads the records of the
forty days after our Lord's resurrection
will see that He is represented as having
been raised to life in His body, but in that
body transformed into a quite new state.
He no longer lives here or there, in Jerusalem or Galilee, so that the disciples could
find Him by calling there. He has not to
pass by walking from one scene to another.
Closed doors are no obstacle to Him. He
seems to be existing on some higher plane
from which He manifests Himself, in
different forms and guises, according to His
spiritual purpose. He can walk with the

two disciples to Emmaus, and even eat
with the eleven in Jerusalem. But we
are not to suppose that He needs food or
depends upon locomotion. It is suggested
in the narratives that He had, on the
morning of the resurrection, left the tomb
before it was opened, and that the body
had passed out of the grave-clothes, leaving them to collapse in their places. All
this corresponds very well with S. Paul's
teaching of a spiritual body—a body which
is no longer the "flesh and blood" of our
present experience, but has been trans-
muted into a higher state: still material,
but sublimated in such sense that its matter
is no longer the restraining and hamper-
ing medium that we now know, but the
perfect instrument and vehicle of the
spiritual will.

Our Lord's own resurrection is spoken
of by S. Paul as "the resurrection of the
dead" (in the plural), because His resurrection is the foretaste and assurance of
the destiny of all men. He is the Man—
our real representative. In His resurrection we see the issue of life for all of us
who belong to Him. This is a common-
place of the New Testament.

There are three further remarks which
I should wish to make about the Christian
doctrine of immortality.

1. As to the basis on which it rests. It
rests on moral considerations raised to the
point of certain conviction by the resurrection of our Lord. Nothing is more certain
than that, if the supreme and only governor
of the world is a perfectly just and good
God, we do not see the end of His opera-
tions upon individuals or upon society in
this world. It must be that "the more
parts of His works are hid," and the fulfilment of justice and righteousness is not
seen on ,this side of death. The most
extreme instance of this incompleteness
would be the life of Christ ending at Calvary in consummate failure and shame.
There must be, we feel, something more.
And the other moral argument is equally
forcible. ·If there be an eternal God
who raises men into intimate communion
with Himself, it cannot be imagined that
He will leave the human person who has
been allowed to become His friend to
perish like a worm. We watch a good old
man's faculties failing, his faculties physical
and intellectual. But there is something
which shows no signs of failing—that is
the assurance of communion with God
and the quiet confidence that beyond death
he is going to a still more intimate fellowship with his divine friend. These and
the like considerations have made the

belief in immortality seem inseparable from the higher kind of faith in God. It is this sort of longing confidence which first the teaching of Christ and then His resurrection confirmed. It is in this sense that S. Paul declares that God "brought life and incorruption to light through the gospel."

2. It must never be forgotten that that ancient people amongst whom our faith was developed, as we believe under divine leading, were definitely debarred by their laws from what we call spiritualism. They were not to seek to have dealings with the dead. We should be loath indeed to limit scientific curiosity or to deny the lawfulness of any kind of serious investigation into facts. But spiritualism is very prevalent in our time, and we can watch its effects on men and women over a wide area. It seems to stimulate in them exactly that sort of excitement and curiosity which needs to be repressed, and to tend to a morbid sort of religiousness which is very unlike Christianity. I cannot help often feeling that, if the experiences which spiritualists report are true experiences, it is more likely that they are the victims of clever demons than in real communication with the spirits of just men being made perfect. At any rate it is of the greatest

importance that we should keep it clearly
before men's minds that the Christian's
belief in immortality should follow from
and depend upon his belief in God.

3. No doubt over a large area of Christianity the resurrection of the body has
been supposed to mean that the material
atoms of our present bodies are to be re-col-
lected and become the resurrection bodies.
This to a more scientific age is inconceivable, and the appeal to divine omnipotence
is very unsatisfying. So it is a comfort to
feel that some early Christian thinkers
held a more reasonable view, and that this
rather than the cruder belief is suggested
by S. Paul in his treatment of the resurrection.[1] He there contemplates three sorts
of resurrection. There is the resurrection
of Christ on the third day, which we must
suppose to have involved the transformation of His dead body in the tomb into
the spiritual body of His resurrection.
Secondly, there is the sudden transformation "in a moment, in the twinkling of an
eye, at the last trump," of those whom the
last day shall find alive. This he speaks
of as "a mystery," doubtless remembering
that "we see through a glass darkly" the
experiences of the last day. Intermediate
between these two he speaks of the resur-

[1] In 1 Cor. xv.

rection of those who had fallen asleep in
Christ, and whose bodies had "seen
corruption."

Specially in view of their case he con-
ceives that the earlier "natural" bodies
were, to speak in a figure, the seeds of
the spiritual bodies that should be. Death
and corruption, while it dissolves the
natural body, enables God to give to each
his own proper spiritual body. This suggests a continuous personal identity, but it
does not suggest the re-collection of material
particles. It makes us prefer the phrase
the "resurrection of the body" or "of the
dead" to the phrase the "resurrection of
the flesh"; for "flesh and blood," S. Paul
says, "shall not inherit the kingdom of
God." But it leaves us with the assurance
that perfected manhood in us, as in Christ,
shall have its perfect spiritual organ and
expression, its spiritual body.

JUDGEMENT AND HELL

We have spoken of the blessed dead;
but there is another and an awful side to
our belief about the end. It is not the
idea of our religion that "we are all going
to the same place." Life is represented to
us in the Bible, and nowhere with more
penetrating simplicity than in our Lord's

teaching, as an awful choice between two
alternatives. We are always choosing life
or death, light or darkness, good or evil.
By choosing the evil or the darkness we
pass under divine judgement. Judgement
on the evil choice is not to be considered
as an arbitrary act of God, but as the
inevitable consequence of the choice itself.
Acts form habits, and habits stereotype
into a settled character which becomes
more and more fixed. And if the character be determined by lust or pride or
hatred or falsehood, if these things become
the man's real self, death does not change
him. The awfulness of death is that it
does not change us, but only sets us naked
and bare in the presence of the holiness
of God.

In a famous passage of Isaiah the
coming of God to Israel in His awful holiness is described by the metaphor of fire.
The sinners in Zion are afraid. "Who
among us," they cry, "shall dwell with
the devouring fire? Who among us shall
dwell with everlasting burnings?" The
answer is that only the righteous man can
dwell with God. God cannot change
Himself. He cannot take the character
which has become determined for evil
into union with Himself. He is indeed
infinitely merciful, but He cannot save

us in spite of ourselves. That is the terrible prerogative of our freedom. And if words mean anything we are assured by our Lord and His apostles that obstinate refusal of the light, obstinate adherence to the wrong, may bring the soul to a spiritual ruin so complete as to become final and irreversible. I do not think it is possible to attach any other sense to the tremendous language of the New Testament.

Our Lord means us to take this warning to ourselves, rather than to inquire about others. But hell, since there is a hell, becomes part of the scene of the future, and must be fitted somehow into our whole picture of the universe as it shall be. The last judgement, which is depicted in tremendous imagery, leaves men divided into "saved" and "lost."

There has been a vigorous reaction against the "old-fashioned" teaching of hell. This was in part quite legitimate, for God had been represented by current Calvinism as creating multitudes of men irreversibly doomed to hell from their creation, and even more generally as condemning to hell those who, through no fault of their own, had failed to believe and be baptized—even the heathen, for instance, who had never heard of Christ,

and unbaptized infants, who had no capacity for choice.   Now we who believe in
Christ know nothing more certainly than
the character of God.   We know that He
is perfect love, perfect equity.   We are
quite justified in refusing to believe about
Him anything which would be inconsistent
with the highest goodness that we can
conceive.   We can be quite sure that He
will do the best possible for every soul
whom He has created.   And we know
that He has worlds beyond this—ages of
ages—in which He can carry out His
hitherto unfulfilled designs.   Any idea
of souls destined for hell by an irreversible
decree of God we may quite dismiss out
of our horizon.   "God will have all men
to be saved, and to come to the knowledge
of the truth."

Thus, if souls are to be lost, it must
be through their own fault.   Those who
have had no opportunity can be supplied
with opportunity, we must suppose, in
some unknown world.   Of course the
Bible is written for those who have
opportunity.   For them indeed "now is
the accepted time; now is the day of
salvation"; and they have no right to
expect another opportunity if they reject
this one.   But we are glad to notice that
S. Peter speaks confidently of our Lord

in Hades as preaching the Gospel to the
dead, with the intention that, though they
were judged according to men in the
flesh, they might live according to God
in the spirit.[1] And we rightly resent
on behalf of the church the closing of
any avenue of hope which the Divine
Spirit has not closed, and the preten-
sion to any fuller knowledge than in
fact is given to us.

If I am to lay down definite conclusions I
should say—(1) that the universalism which
is so popular to-day—the belief that every
created spirit must ultimately be recovered
to fulfil the end of its being in God, though
it is supported by some early Christian
authorities, and though it has never been
formally condemned by the church with
any ecumenical judgement, is flatly contrary, plainly contrary, to the language
used by our Lord about the destinies of
men, and generally to the language of the
New Testament.

(2) That I do not think that, by exclud-
ing universalism, we are absolutely shut
up into the almost intolerable belief in
unending conscious torment for the lost.
The language of the Bible does not necessarily suggest this.[2] I do not think that it

[1] 1 S. Pet. iii. 19 ; iv. 6.
[2] The only phrase which expresses the idea clearly is
Rev. xx. 10. There it refers to the beast and the false

supplies us with any ground for the dogma
that the consciousness of a man once
created is indestructible.   Final moral
ruin may involve, I cannot but think,
such a dissolution of personality as carries
with it the cessation of personal consciousness.   In this way the final ruin of
irretrievably lost spirits, awful as it is to
contemplate, may be found consistent with
S. Paul's anticipation of a universe in
which ultimately God is to be all in all—
which does not seem to be really com-
patible with the existence of a region of
everlastingly tormented and rebellious
spirits ; while at the same time the awful
warnings of our Lord and his apostles as
to the inevitable consequences of wilful
final sin supply to every one who chooses
to think at all a most powerful motive to
prefer any effort to the risk of "losing his
own soul."

THE INTERMEDIATE STATE AND PURGATORY

It is certainly the case that the revelation
of the New Testament is not given us to
satisfy our curiosity or to let us feel that
we know or can know the future state

prophet, confessedly symbolical figures, as well as to the
devil.   And in this book all the measures of time are
symbolical.

otherwise than "in part." What is told us is sufficient to make faith firm and hope active, and (we must add) to strengthen the natural fears of an evil conscience—but certainly not to enable us to anticipate the experience of another world. Certainly the final bliss of man is identified with the kingdom which is to come after the end of the world and the day of judgement; and we are led to believe in an intermediate state of (in some sense) disembodied souls, in a condition of waiting or expectancy, following on the "particular judgement"—that is, the disclosure of a man's real state which appears to be associated with each one's death. About this intermediate state we are told exceedingly little, but we are led to suppose that there is such a state both for good and bad, and that it is a state of conscious life, and for those who have departed in Christ a state of greater nearness to Him, a being "in Christ" and "with Christ."

It is a state where the souls of just men are made perfect. There is infinite satisfaction about such phrases. But how much they are allowed to know about us who remain on earth, and about the incidents of earth, we are not informed. Nor can we tell at all what the lapse of

time, as we know it, may mean to them.
It was one view held in the early church
that souls at death are made suddenly
and instantaneously perfect for good or
evil. But this idea has not proved acceptable. We almost all instinctively tend to
believe in some sort of purgatory, a state
of cleansing and gradual emancipation
and enlightenment for the imperfect.
As regards any such purgatorial state,
however, we must confess that the New
Testament is absolutely silent.[1] S. Augustine allows it with a "perhaps." And we
cannot get beyond that. It is rather a
conclusion of our natural reason than
a revealed truth. And inasmuch as the
Roman church is specially identified with
the teaching of purgatory, it is important
to notice that the ameliorative aspect of
purgatory is not that on which the Roman
church has laid stress. According to the
Roman doctrine, though all bad habits
and vicious inclinations of the soul be
instantly purified away by the moment-
ary fire of the particular judgement, or
the accompanying vision of God, and
though the soul be rendered instantly
fit for heaven, yet it is detained in pain

---

[1] S. Paul's much-quoted words (1 Cor. iii. 12–15)
about a man "being saved, yet so as by fire," have
really nothing to do with the matter.

simply to work out the temporal punishment due to its sins. The Roman purgatory
is thus predominantly penal or vindictive.
What we moderns desire is the purgatory,
penal indeed, but predominantly educa-
tive and ameliorative, which certain great
Christian teachers have imagined. In
that we may—nay, I feel, we must—
believe; but it is rather a conclusion of
our reasoning than a part of what is
revealed.

THE COMMUNION OF SAINTS

This article of belief was added as an
expansion of the article about the holy
catholic church. It means that all the
redeemed, living and departed, are in one
fellowship, which death does not interrupt.
The visible catholic church is only a part
of the whole church. Only the lower
limbs of the body of Christ are visible to
us. We are in communion also with the
dead, "with the spirits of just men made
perfect"; and we are not prohibited from
adding—with the spirits of just men being
made perfect. How are we to exercise
this fellowship?

There can be no real question that in
the Middle Ages a superstructure of largely
rotten material but of very portentous

weight had been built upon the basis of the belief in the communion of saints. Current ideas about purgatory and indulgences and invocation of saints, and current practices based on these ideas, were most urgently in need of amendment and reform. But the reaction of Protestantism was culpably unguarded, and the Church of England shared in this lamentable reaction, so that, in result, we almost forgot in our practical and public religion our continued fellowship with the blessed dead. One may question whether mediaeval superstitions have not been preferable to our blank ignoring of the communion of the saints. We must aim at living without superstition, but also in the full light of truth. And the communion of saints, as its name implies, is pre-eminently a matter for public recognition and not merely private memory.

There are in particular two expressions of the communion of saints on the restoration of which in our common as well as our private worship we ought to insist.

1. We must recover without apology or concealment the practice of prayer for the dead. It is matter of revelation that the departed are alive and waiting their final perfection. They need something as we need something. And therefore we may

pray for them. That is a practice inevitably resulting from the revealed belief
about the efficacy of prayer for others in
all their real needs. I should contend
that S. Paul prayed for his dead friend
Onesiphorus.[1] I am sure that the church
has always prayed for the dead, for light
and refreshment and peace, and that they
may receive forgiveness and mercy of the
Lord. I do not want to define. But I
must insist upon my right to pray, leaving
all unknown things in God's hands. And
I must demand this right, by legitimate
authority, in the public services.

2. Besides praying for our dead generally, besides keeping again our All Souls'
Day, we should remember specially the
heroes of our faith, those whom in a
special sense we call saints. The ancient
church used to commemorate them
solemnly by name. Moreover, believing
that nothing could be more practically
certain than that the perfected spirits were
occupied in properly spiritual activity, and
that their larger love, in the unseen world,
must lead them to pray for us who remain
in this world, the ancient church desired
to have them for its intercessors, and
solemnly asked God that it might be
allowed to benefit by their intercessions.

[1] 2 Tim. i. 18.

o

S. Cyril of Jerusalem speaks thus of
the commemoration of the dead, which
in his days followed the consecration of the eucharist. "Afterwards we
make mention also of those who have
fallen asleep, first of patriarchs, prophets,
apostles, martyrs, that God by their
prayers and intercessions will receive
our supplications.   Then also (we pray)
on behalf of our holy fathers and bishops,
and generally of all those who have fallen
asleep amongst us, believing that there
will be the greatest benefit to the souls
of those on whose behalf our prayer is
offered up while the holy and tremendous
sacrifice is amongst us." [1]

I should earnestly wish to see restored
amongst us the public commemoration, as
in the First Prayer Book, of " the wonderful grace and virtue, declared in all Thy
saints from the beginning of the world:
and chiefly in the glorious and most
blessed Virgin Mary, mother of Thy Son
Jesus Christ our Lord and God, and in
the holy patriarchs, prophets, apostles, and
martyrs"; and I would have this general
commemoration accompanied not only as
in the First Book, by direct prayers for
the dead generally, but also by a specific
request to God that we may be allowed

[1] *Catechesis myst.* v. 9.

the benefit of the intercession of the saints.

This has been called comprecation. But the main body of the church, since the fifth century of its life, has not been satis-fied without directly asking the saints for their prayers (invocation), though it was long before these direct invocations were admitted into the public services. As to this I do not feel that anything could be more natural; but it cannot be denied that, to sustain it, we need the assurance that we can have direct access to the saints, and that they can directly hear us ; and it is exactly this which the church, by the admissions of its theologians, is not authorized to give us. The theologians of the mediaeval church tell us only that the saints are allowed to see us and our needs in God ; which I suppose may be expressed in other words by saying that, if we cannot get at them to address them directly, yet we can be sure that God will disclose to them what He sees fit that they should know. But, if this is so, it would seem to follow that we had better make our prayers to God that He will be pleased to let the saints know our needs and let us profit by their prayers. The instinct of invocation, however, has been wide-spread and almost irresistible. It is not

only Romish : for the Christians of the
East use it as much as the Christians of
the West. They address with familiar
confidence not only the famous saints but
their own departed friends. Certainly we
are not called upon to forbid such invocation. But the sense of what is not revealed
to us should restrain our use of it, even
in private, and, following the practice of
the ancient church, we should admit into
our public services no prayers but those
addressed to God.

CHAPTER VI

Christian Morality

PREOCCUPATION with the dead and curiosity about the world of the dead must, if we are to judge by a Biblical standard, be pronounced morbid features in religion. The New Testament gives us indeed the most complete assurance about the state and prospects of "them that are fallen asleep," and the abiding sense of communion with them; but information about their state is given us with such reserve as to direct our faculties towards this world, which really lies open before us, and which God has given into our charge. Thus the unworldliness of Christians is to make them only more effective in the world. God is to be first in their lives—in unquestioned and undisputed supremacy; but they are to test the reality of their love of God only by their conduct towards their fellow men. Their manner of life is to be heavenly; it is to draw all its motives and power from that heavenly place where Christ is seated at the right hand of God,

it is to measure everything by the issues of
eternal life and eternal death ; but all this
"other-worldliness," so far from making
them indifferent to this world, is only to
make them feel the importance of everything that happens in this world, because
of its divine origin and eternal issues.
And it is the spectacle of what Christians
are in the life which they share with all
other men which, by its moral attractive-
ness, is to draw men to Christ: that
"wherein they speak against you as
evil-doers, they may by your good works,
which they shall behold, glorify God in
the day of visitation."[1]

Thus we come to consider Christian
morality or ethics—the principles of Christian life, individual and social. And, of
course, we must make our beginning from
Him who sets the standard for Christians
—from Jesus Christ our Lord.

THE MIND OF CHRIST

What we have to consider is the spirit
of our Lord's human life and teaching.
Great mistakes have been made through
forgetting both what our Lord, in the place
in history which He filled, was able to
assume, and also what He deliberately

[1] 1 S. Pet. ii. 12.

refused to anticipate. Forgetting these considerations, very different classes of people have argued, mistakenly as I think, from the silence of Christ. "He never occupied Himself with social legislation or reform," says one group; "therefore the Christian church ought not to do so." "He said nothing to inspire patriotism or to justify war, and much to require personal meekness and non-resistance," says another group; "and therefore no Christian can rightly be a soldier." "He said nothing about church building or religious ceremonial; therefore," says yet another group, "it is not really proper for the Christian to be much occupied in the external organization of worship." But all these groups of people who use the same arguments from different points of view forget what is of great importance. Our Lord assumes not only the lofty personal morality but also the social order of the Old Testament, to which he ascribes divine authority, and which was full of detailed social legislation and social instruction. What He sets Himself to do within the Jewish people is to restore and perfect the spirit which lies behind legislation—the spirit of humanity. And, so far as He contemplated the future, He seems deliberately to have abstained from

making laws for His disciples in the main ;
but He intends His society to legislate in
His own name and Spirit after He should
have gone out of sight.   And He said,
"He that heareth you heareth Me."[1]

Again, war will doubtless cease when
the mass of men are really, even if
imperfectly, Christians.   For their inter-
national fellowship will then be based
on something better than selfishness, individual or corporate.   But meanwhile
each nation has a vocation and a divine
right to exist.   In the recent memory of
Israel, when our Lord came, the Macca-
bees had been their national heroes, who
had fought for their national existence
when it was threatened, and had waged
a great war of self-defence.   Every pa-
triotic Israelite gloried in them.   There
is not the slightest reason to think that
our Lord would have repudiated them ;
and, though He made it evident that
political independence was not now the
vocation of Israel, there is no reason to
think He would have forbidden a nation
which had received the faith He came to
impart to defend its boundaries against
invaders or assist in defending some other
nation.   Our Lord does indeed repudiate
pride and corporate selfishness, and re-

[1] S. Luke x. 16.

quires us to love our neighbours as ourselves. This is to repudiate a great deal that has paraded itself as patriotism in human history. But there is a true patriotism which believes in the divine purpose for each nation, and cannot, for the sake of all, allow the insolent aggression of others upon its legitimate liberty. It seems to me to be idle to argue from what our Lord says about personal submission to injuries that He would have refused to allow a man to defend either his wife and children or his country.

Once more, ceremonial observances belong to human nature everywhere. "Duties of religion," says Richard Hooker, "performed by whole societies of men ought to have in them a sensible excellency correspondent to the majesty of Him whom we worship." Our Lord shows not the slightest antipathy to the religious ceremonialism of Israel. There is not a word against it. He condemns not forms but empty forms. When His own redemptive action had so deeply changed the basis of religious observance, it would be the function of His church to provide for suitable religious ceremonial. Meanwhile He contents Himself with refashioning the spirit of worship as of human life generally.

How shall we seek to describe the moral spirit of Jesus?

1. He bases morality in the heart and will. Every settled society must have legislation both negative and positive in order to protect itself, and such legislation is concerned exclusively with outward acts. For the Jews this legislation had a divine sanction. Moreover every settled society develops standards of respectability which its public opinion sedulously maintains. Nowhere was this more marked than in Jewish society. But our Lord absolutely refuses to be content with such external standards. He insists on forcing back the standards of personal purity and mutual duty into the inner sphere of motive and desire—into the heart of man, which only God can see. He would have us regard the deliberate will to commit adultery as equivalent to the act itself; and the first movement of anger in the heart as a sin deserving of punishment; and He carries back the sin of swearing falsely till its correction is found in a universal truthfulness. He will not allow that outward observances can be the source of moral defilement, but only the inward will of the heart. This He applies equally to all the three aspects of morality—our duty to God, our duty to

ourselves, and our duty to our neighbour; and to the corresponding kinds of religious action—to prayer, fasting, and almsgiving. The real value of each lies in the inner region where "your Father seeth in secret."

2. It follows from this that our Lord would have us intensely alive to the perils of living by public opinion. He is for ever pointing out its defectiveness and its blinding effect upon the conscience. The Pharisees, for instance, were intensely conscientious, only their conscience was blinded to the most important considerations by their tradition. "Thus have ye made the word of God of none effect because of your tradition." "How can ye believe which receive glory one of another, and the glory that cometh from the only God ye seek not?" "Take heed that the light that is in you be not darkness."[1] This is a tremendously important consideration. Respectability is not morality.

Every society in the pursuit of its own ideals tends to draw a distinction between the sins which are disreputable, and merit social reprobation, and those for which there is easy condonation, or which can even be taken for granted. Our Lord will have no such distinction. He carries

[1] S. Matt. xv. 6; S. John v. 44; S. Luke xi. 35.

sin back to the heart, to the inner relation of a man to God and his neighbour, and He will have no distinction between respectable and disreputable sins. No one can accuse our Lord of laxity as to sexual sins. But He will never suffer us to consider the sins of the flesh, or other sins which make a man disreputable, as if they were worse than covetousness or selfishness or pride which are consistent with respectability. Indeed our Lord's deepest indignation is expressed towards the sins of the Pharisees who stood highest in public estimation. This refusal to recognize any moral distinction between respectable and disreputable sins strikes a tremendous blow at the current morality of almost any settled society, especially if it be religious.

3. If all real morality lies in a right relation to God in the heart, everything depends on the right idea of God. Our Lord was for ever declaring His fatherhood, His equal love and care for every one of His children. Here we get to the heart of our Lord's moral teaching and practice. He "hid not Himself from His own flesh." He dealt with every one, however much an outcast from respectable society, with an equal regard. He loved every man. Though His

special mission was only to Israel, He made it quite plain that this was only a temporary limitation. He welcomed the faith which he found in the Roman centurion and the Syrophenician woman. His love knew no limits. His compassion went out towards every one's need. He approached every one with the respect due to manhood and womanhood. He made no account of wealth or intellect or social importance. He treated things which give men privileged positions as if they were positive obstacles to their entrance into the kingdom. He did not think of God as if He were all mildness. He proclaimed the wrath of God as well as His mercy. But the wrath of God and His own wrath is specially directed against the insolence which despises others and which ignores the infinite worth of every human soul. "Take heed that ye despise not one of these little ones." "It is not the will of your Father which is in heaven that one of these little ones should perish." "It were better for a man that a millstone should be hanged about his neck, and that he should be drowned in the depths of the sea, than that he should cause one of these little ones to stumble."[1]

4. Thus our Lord's moral teaching

S. Matt. xviii. 10, 14 ; S. Luke xvii. 2.

centres in the profound assertion of God's fatherhood and the equal claim of all His children. His morality is a positive enthusiasm for humanity — for every man as such. That is love; and love carries with it humility, which is the frankest recognition of the equal claim of every one upon life—the absolute refusal to exalt oneself at the expense of another, or to use any other as an instrument for one's own profit. The true spirit of man is the joy of service; and the poorest and weakest, because they need our service more, are to have the first claim upon it. Thus over every awakened soul our Lord seems to stand eliciting, welcoming, and blessing the offer of self-sacrifice. Love, humility, service, and sacrifice—these are the things which characterize His life, and which He would have to be the heart and centre of the life of His disciples. This is the spirit in which we are to co-operate with the will of our Father which is in heaven. It is not too much to say that our Lord first really discovered and disclosed to men the power to lift and redeem which lies hid in compassion— compassion which is wholly without contempt, compassion which has power in it, because it rests upon and is inspired by the compassion of God.

THE ETHICS OF THE EPISTLES

The Epistles of the New Testament are perfect expressions of the mind of Christ. In them, all alike, we have a wonderful belief in the capacity of every individual. The gift of the Holy Spirit, which is the possession of each member of Christ, is the gift of liberty and sonship—liberty meaning the power of self-control, the control of the passions and appetites by the Spirit-enabled will, and also the capacity for intelligent co-operation with the purpose of God in the church and in the world. But this individual liberty is realized by each only as a member of the body in which the law of mutual service enriches each with the gifts of all and binds them together in brotherhood. The Christian Church is "the body" or "the brotherhood," because here only, where the Spirit dwells, can men realize in sonship to God the brotherhood which is meant for all. The principle of brotherhood means that there is to be asked of each the utmost service which each can render, and that there should be given to each according to his need, because if one member suffer, or is in want, the weakness or suffering of each is the weakening of the whole body. Suffering indeed will be the lot of the whole body and of every member of it, but not the misery of being forgotten or despised by the brotherhood ; so that through all afflictions which they share with Christ, their Master and Head, a spirit of rejoicing, a "spirit of glory and of God," rests upon them.

We need to read afresh S. Paul, S. James, S. John, S. Peter, to see with fresh eyes how much of the real glory of Christian ethics we have left out of our mental picture.   The whole spirit of Christian morality is not the glorification of the individual but the sociable spirit of the community.   The ethics of the New Testament are social ethics.   And, in-asmuch as fellowship amongst a number of naturally divergent temperaments lays a great strain on the forbearance of each, the test of sincerity in Christian belief is found in the capacity for cheerful membership.

There is no doubt that it was the love of Christians for one another—the care of all for each—which was one chief cause of the rapid spread of the church.   Men were drawn out of a loveless world into that warm and comfortable fellowship. Equally there is no doubt that it is just this spirit which could win men to-day. One of the most thoughtful of those who have written about our soldiers on the field of battle bears witness to the spirit of brotherliness — unselfishness, generosity, cheerfulness, and humility—which possesses them; but adds significantly that they never think of this as having any connection with religion, with Christianity. "This is surely nothing short of tragedy. Here are men who believed absolutely in the Christian virtues of unselfishness, generosity, charity, and humility, without ever connecting them in their minds with Christ; and, at the same time, what they did associate with Christianity was just on a par with the formalism and smug self-righteousness which Christ spent His whole life in trying to destroy."[1] That is the melancholy fact. We have let charity come to mean something different from brotherly and sisterly love. We have let it become associated with the idea of the patronage of the inferior by the superior. We have allowed men to say that they want "not charity, but justice"—as if charity were anything else than justice perfected.

What we must ask of Churchmen is to bathe themselves again in the spirit of the New Testament and to set themselves so

[1] *A Student in Arms*, pp. 117-18. London: Andrew Melrose. 1916.

Q

resolutely to reproduce it, that "eccle-siastical" shall once again come to mean brotherly.

In our idea of duty—in our idea of the sacraments—in our doctrine of the Spirit, among Catholics and among Protestants we have suffered an excessive individualism to obliterate or hide much that is most essential and central in Christian ethics.

THE TEN COMMANDMENTS

I cannot but think that this is partly due among ourselves to the over-prominent place which has been assigned in our Prayer Book to the Ten Commandments. Nowhere in ancient Christendom or in modern catholicism outside our own limits have the Ten Commandments been given so dominant a position. There is no doubt that they had behind them the authority of God as a code of elementary law for the people of Israel. There is no doubt that they set the ancient people of God upon the right lines. The fundamental principles of human society, and the true principles of ethics are to be found there. Interpreted as our Lord interprets them they can become a code for Christians; but the interpretation is a very thorough transformation. "Thou shalt not take the name of the Lord thy God in vain"

becomes the profound duty of truthfulness; "thou shalt do no murder" becomes the law of love; and "thou shalt
not commit adultery" the law of purity
in thought and desire. They are transformed, in fact, from negative into positive
precepts. They all admit of this sort of
transformation. But simply proclaimed
from the altar they are not understood
in this new sense. That God is against
the sinner—that they make us feel with
trembling. But they are, as they stand,
negative precepts—"thou shalt not"—and
they give an unduly negative appearance
to Christian morality. They forbid certain vicious actions or tempers, and allow
us to be satisfied if these particular offences
are avoided. And some of them are pro-
hibitions which in their original sense no
longer hold. We are no longer prohibited,
like the Jews in the second commandment, from all representations of created
things even in connection with worship.
The incarnation of the Son of God has
hallowed Christian art in our churches;
and sacred pictures have become "the
books of the unlearned." And the Christian Sunday, the Lord's Day, is certainly
not simply the Jewish sabbath transferred
to another day.

Of course our Catechism does give a

very liberal interpretation to the Ten Commandments. Let us listen to it.

"What dost thou chiefly learn by these commandments?

"I learn two things: my duty towards God, and my duty towards my neighbour.

"What is thy duty towards God?

"My duty towards God is to believe in Him, to fear Him, and to love Him, with all my heart, with all my mind, with all my soul, and with all my strength;[1] to worship Him, to give Him thanks, to put my whole trust in Him, to call upon Him,[2] to honour His holy name and His word,[3] and to serve Him truly all the days of my life.[4]

"What is thy duty towards thy neighbour?

"My duty towards my neighbour, is to love him as myself, and to do to all men, as I would they should do unto me: to love, honour, and succour my father and mother: to honour and obey the king, and all that are put in authority under him: to submit myself to all my governors, teachers, spiritual pastors and masters: to order myself lowly and reverently to all my betters:[5] to hurt nobody by word nor deed: to be true and just in all my

---

[1] First Commandment.   [2] Second.   [3] Third.
        [4] Fourth.   [5] Fifth.

dealing : to bear no malice nor hatred in my heart :[1] to keep my hands from picking and stealing,[2] and my tongue from evil-speaking, lying, and slandering :[3] to keep my body in temperance, soberness, and chastity :[4] not to covet nor desire other men's goods ; but to learn and labour truly to get mine own living, and to do my duty in that state of life, unto which it shall please God to call me." [5]

This indeed is a transformed version of the Ten Commandments. But very few of our communicants have it in their mind. Even the questions in some books of self-examination which interpret the Ten Commandments present a too negative impression of Christian duty. Thus I cannot but wish that the Ten Command-ments might be publicly recited in church only occasionally, and then with their properly Christian interpretation, while some more easily intelligible summary of Christian morals [6] were in the minds and memories of all our members.

[1] Sixth. [2] Eighth. [3] Ninth. [4] Seventh. [5] Tenth.
[6] The summary in the Catechism would probably suffice if the statement of the duty of subordinates to superiors were there balanced by an equally simple statement of the corresponding duties of those in any kind of authority or position of advantage. As it stands we cannot deny that it produces a feeling of unfairness. A reference to *Murray's Dictionary* will show that "betters" cannot be interpreted to mean "those better than ourselves."

THE AUTHORITY OF THE CHURCH

I began by speaking of what our Lord assumed—He assumed the State and the authority of the State. Speaking as an Israelite He assumed the legislation of the Law and the social teaching of the prophets. But if the Jewish State had continued in being and had accepted the teaching of Christ He would have infused into the old legislation and the old moral teaching a new spirit, which would have profoundly modified it. As things actually happened the Jewish people rejected Christ, and the Christian church started on its career wholly divorced from the nation of its origin ; and for some centuries of its life in the Roman Empire it was almost wholly debarred from political action. Its only concern was with the moral discipline of its own members. But so soon as the church in any city or nation rises to a position of political influence, there must arise a new conception of Christian civic duty. Of this important aspect of Christian ethics I shall have to speak in a later chapter. But we cannot think rightly about Christian morality at all without bringing into view the social discipline which the church was intended to exercise, and did exercise from the first, over

its own members. Except in the single
matter of marriage, on which our Lord
appears to have laid down a law,[1] He
abstained from anything like legislation
for His church. He expressed in His
teaching extraordinarily luminous moral
ideas and ideals of duty. But He left it
to His church to apply these ideals and
ideas in a system of moral discipline, and
He gave to the church a divine authority
to exercise this discipline. There was not
in the church from its beginning any doubt
about this.

Thus the New Testament presents us
with a picture, which later church history
only elaborates, of a corporate body legis-
lating for its members with a divine
sanction. The normal Christian is a man
under authority — the authority of the
body he belongs to. In his whole life
he ought to feel this corporate authority,
and he ought to recognize in detail "the
precepts of the church." We know the
causes which brought about the great
rebellion against church authority which
is called the Reformation. Over parts of
Europe the church of the papal obedience
reasserted its sway, and a much stricter
discipline was inaugurated. The stricter

[1] 1 Cor. vii. 10, "Not I, but the Lord." He speaks,
however, as one restoring not originating a law.

discipline was in theological and ecclesiastical matters rather than in morality. Still, the individual Churchman knew that he must obey the precepts of the church. With us the unhappy fusion of Church and State brought about a situation in which the church was hardly recognized as having any authority apart from the State. And now that the State has ceased to act as the guardian of a distinctively Christian morality the individual churchman is allowed to remain with hardly any consciousness of being under obedience to a body which represents Christ. I would give only two examples of this startling deficiency.

The mediaeval church possessed a noble and carefully formulated tradition of social and political ethics—for instance, a really Christian doctrine of property, limiting the rights of property by considerations of the general welfare and of the authority of God. But a philosophy of individual self-interest arose and became dominant, especially in England. It mastered the legislature; and our laws came to care more about the rights of property than the rights of persons, and to push the rights of property to such a point as admitted of little regard being paid to the interests of the community, and especially of its less for-

tunate members—those "who have not."
And, in spite of the prevalence of this
frankly unchristian theory and practice, the
church corporately was silent. Christians
were at liberty to make money out of slum-
dwellings, degrading to their inhabitants;
or to sweat their workpeople; or to invest
their capital in commercial enterprises
without any regard to the good of mankind—without regard to any other consideration except the return they would
get for their money: and all this in flat
defiance of Christian principles, without
the church ever seriously warning them
that they were guilty of something like a
moral apostasy.

I must give one other example. A
generation ago it began to be known that
by the use of certain expedients it was
possible and even easy for men and women
to gratify their sexual appetites without
the trouble, expense, and pain involved
in the procreation of children. The
general verdict of the Christian conscience, where it is at pains to be
instructed, condemns such practices as a
degradation of marriage and of the sexual
relation, severing its inherent pleasure
from the conditions which ennoble and
restrain it. The Roman Catholic church
and the Jewish community made their

R

condemnation of these practices more or
less effective, and within the limits of their
influence they were kept in restraint. But
outside these communions they have been
allowed to gain a fearful prevalence without any organized or public expression of
the judgement of the church.

These are instances of a very serious
neglect. The conscience of a man is not
the voice of God, but a faculty which
enables him to keep in touch with God's
moral will, as his reason enables him to
keep in touch with truth. Both, if they are
to be effective, need education. Among
the means of educating the conscience of
Christians none should be more obvious
than the voice of the church. A Christian
is meant to live in the light of the judgement of the divine society of which he is
a member. And the church which neglects to enlighten and guide and warn its
members on moral questions neglects a
vital part of its duty.

Even in minor matters it is necessary
and wholesome that members of the
church should feel their obligation to
observe the precepts of the church. It
keeps them in mind of their membership,
it strengthens their spirit of discipline ;
and if the precepts are sound it keeps
them in the right way. Whether the

precepts of the Roman Church are wholly good I need not discuss ; at least we recognize what an advantage it is to a Roman Catholic that he knows, as we say, "exactly what he has got to do." And it is the intention of the Church of England that we should live under like precepts. Thus—(1) the duty of public worship, especially on Sundays and other holy days ; (2) the duty of hearing and reading Holy Scripture ; (3) the duty of communicating at least three times a year ; (4) the duty of almsgiving and of paying church dues; (5) the duty of not marrying within the prohibited degrees ; (6) the duty of keeping the fast and feast days of the church ; (7) the duty of making one's will—are duties which the Church of England in its Prayer Book and canons lays upon its members.[1] Some of us would desire a revision of these rules, at least so as to make attendance at the Lord's own service the normal obligation of the Lord's Day. But, be the rules never so good, they fail of their object unless they are practically understood of all, and unless the church makes it evident that it intends they should be observed. With-

[1] Upon its clergy only it lays the duty of the daily recitation of Morning and Evening Prayer in public or private. It would have made a vast difference if this had never been forgotten.

out such precepts of the church, universally known and loyally accepted within
our membership, we shall never have
anything approaching to a healthy church-
manship; and such practical recognition of
membership is an important part of the
moral discipline of Christianity.

THE EVANGELICAL COUNSELS

Finally, a word must be said about the
"counsels" or special vocations for some,
as well as about the moral duties of all.
Purity, self-control, charity, self-sacrifice,
humility—these and the like virtues are
incumbent upon all. But some, not all,
our Lord called to be apostles and evangelists, pastors and missionaries, and He
gave them special injunctions to secure
their entire detachment from worldly
cares. Further he set before some, not
all, the counsel of voluntary poverty:
"Go and sell all that thou hast, and come
and follow me." And He also suggested
as a vocation for some, not for all, deliberate virginity. These last calls, welcomed
and acted upon, have been the foundation
of what is specially called the "religious
state." And because these ascetic vocations pursued individually lead to all kinds
of perilous eccentricities the church has

joined to the vocations of poverty and chastity the vocation of obedience to a superior and a common rule, in order to keep the Religious State sane and healthy.

Thus the church has honoured the special vocation of those who consecrate their lives under the three vows of poverty, chastity, and obedience; and there are very few things in the Church of England for which we need more heartily to give thanks than for the revival amongst us of this special vocation, both among men and women. There is a very difficult theological question about the "merit" of "works of supererogation"— that is, good works, such as obedience to these special calls, which are over and above what is required of every one. But I do not propose to discuss this sub-ject here. On the one hand, it cannot be denied that it is very difficult to eliminate the distinction between ordinary require-ments and special merits. It is very difficult to say that any one sins by refus-ing a special call as he would sin by refusing a universal duty. On the other hand, it cannot be denied that the New Testament, especially our Lord's words and S. Paul's, are singularly discour-aging to the idea of acquiring merit; and, to whatever theological system they have belonged, we may rejoice that the heroic saints have, for the most part, been singularly averse to claiming merit for themselves. Meanwhile this at least is certain. No church can strike the imagination of men, or enlist their whole loyalty, unless it affords full scope for the exercise of the more heroic kinds of sacrifice, and gives to such sacrifice frank and corporate honour.

We have at this moment a grand opportunity for proclaiming afresh the true spirit of Christian morality, the gospel of human life. The appalling strife of nations which is drenching in blood so large a part of the world, the threatening strife of classes and many other symptoms of disease in modern life have produced a widespread disillusionment as to the possibilities of any civilization which is based on competitive selfishness, whether it be the selfishness of individuals, of classes, or of nations. Men are yearning for some adequate and stable basis of human fellowship. And it is this that Christianity offers them. Its ethics are frankly supernatural: for it is only by the help of motives and forces drawn from beyond the world that men can subdue their selfish lusts and appetites and become fit for fellowship. But fellowship in the Spirit of God is what Christ offers to men. And while He accepts as a legitimate part of human nature the desire for personal happiness, and frankly bids men strive for eternal rewards, He proclaims deliberate self-sacrifice to be the only road to self-realization, and the only instrument of human redemption.

CHAPTER VII

Prayer

ACCORDING to the teaching of our Lord and of the New Testament generally prayer is to be one of the chief occupations of men. To a certain extent indeed it has been so all the world over. All the world over man appears as a being moving out towards nature to appropriate its resources, and therein lies the history of civilization ; moving out again towards his fellow men to adjust his relations with them, and therein lies the history of society ; but also as a being moving out towards the unseen, towards God or gods, however ignorantly conceived, and therein lies the history of religion. Of this religious development of man the culminating point is to be found in Christ. In Him, as the church believes, is to be found the relation of man to God perfected in sonship. In Him, therefore, is to be found the perfection of prayer. And no one can read the Gospels without seeing that it is our Lord's intention to surround Himself

128

with men of prayer. No one, moreover, can read the Epistles without seeing how diligently the first Christians set themselves to the work of prayer.

Our Lord may be said to have taught His disciples two great lessons with regard to prayer. First, that prayer is efficacious; that is, that asking God, persistently and patiently, is one chief means of obtaining results. Plainly our Lord is interested in, and would have us reverence, all kinds of practical human activity. There are multitudes of things which God means for us and for the world that will never be ours unless we work for them. But also, and quite as truly, there are multitudes of things which God means for us, and through us for our brethren, which will never be ours or theirs unless we pray for them. Prayer produces results. Prayer accomplishes on the earth what nothing else can accomplish. "Ask, and ye shall receive." As "the Lord's brother" says, "Ye have not because ye ask not."[1] Thus our Lord would have His disciples possessed by an unhesitating belief in the efficacy of prayer. And we may lay it to heart that, however great the intellectual difficulties of conceiving the interaction of the divine and human wills, there is no

[1] S. James iv. 2.

intellectual difficulty whatever about the efficacy of prayer which does not apply equally to the efficacy of work. In both directions we are bound to believe that the practical results depend upon our own wills.

But when His disciples had taken in this lesson, there was another which they had to learn, perhaps more difficult—that is, that the efficacy of prayer depends upon our learning to desire and ask what it is the will of God to give. Prayer is not to be an attempt to persuade God to do what He had not intended to do. If we could succeed in doing that, it would be to our loss. Prayer is a method of liberating the hand of God to do what He would do, but cannot do unless we correspond with His will. Intelligent correspondence with the purpose of God—that is the spirit of effective work, and the spirit of all science; and that is the spirit of effective prayer. It is marvellous how many of the objections urged against the reasonableness of praying fall to the ground at once when this principle is really grasped. And inasmuch as in our Lord we really see the mind of God brought near and made intelligible to us, so our praying becomes effective in proportion as we learn to make Christ's mind our mind, and

His desires our desires. This is what I described as the second lesson which our Lord set Himself to teach His disciples about prayer: "If ye abide in me and my words abide in you, ye shall ask what ye will and it shall be done unto you." "Whatsoever ye shall ask the Father in my name, he will give it you. Hitherto have ye asked (so many things in your own name, but) nothing in my name."[1]

It hardly needs saying that to ask in Christ's name means something quite different from adding the words "through Jesus Christ" at the end of our prayers. The ambassador goes abroad "in the name" of king and country, the commercial traveller travels "in the name" of his firm, because he goes to express not his own intentions and wishes, but the intentions and wishes of the greater power behind him which he represents. That is what we mean by praying in the name of Christ. The same idea is really implied in the phrase "Whatsoever ye pray and ask, believe that ye have received it, and ye shall have it": for we cannot really ask with this confident expectation unless we know in sufficient measure the mind of God and our own mind is identified with it.

[1] S. John xv. 7, 16; xvi. 23, 24, 26.

But nowhere is the idea so effectively
expressed as in the Lord's Prayer, which,
indeed, is not one prayer among many,
but the mould and pattern of all praying.
There—in the order no less than the
content of the petitions—is the secret of
prayer in the name of Christ. It begins
with bidding us lay aside our selfishness.
It is "our Father," not "my Father,"
whom I am to approach — the impartial
Father with whom is no respect of persons: "which art in heaven," whose ways
are higher than our ways and His thoughts
than our thoughts, even as the heaven
is higher than the earth, and who yet
bends Himself to the heart of every one of
His children. "Hallowed be Thy name."
Here we are required at once to do
what is most difficult to flesh and blood,
to exalt God's honour above man's need
into the first place in our desires. "Thy
kingdom come, Thy will be done." We
are to merge our little schemes in God's
great purpose, and bend our stubborn wills
into harmony with His. "In earth as it is
in heaven."[1] We are bidden to open our
imagination to the great angelic world of

---

[1] This, in all probability, is intended to refer to all
the three previous clauses—"Hallowed be Thy name,"
as in heaven so on earth; "Thy kingdom come," as in
heaven so on earth; "Thy will be done" as in heaven
so on earth.

free spirits who are always honouring
God with an incessant adoration, amongst
whom the order of the divine kingdom
is perfectly realized, and who have no
other will than God's. Then, only then,
when we have exalted God's honour
above our need, and merged our plans
in His, and bent our wills to His, and
opened our imagination to the vastness
of the spiritual world—only then are we
allowed to express our desires for personal and temporal blessings, and then so
restrictedly: not "Give me to-day what
I should so much wish to have," but
" Give us " one and all alike " to-day our
bread for the coming day"—enough to
keep us in life and activity. And, because
we cannot do God's work unless we are
in His peace, therefore "Forgive us our
trespasses "; and that again, not anyhow,
but according to the fixed law by which
God deals with us as we deal with our
fellow men, "as we have forgiven them
that trespass against us." And because
we are weak and frail, "Lead us not into
temptation (or trial), but deliver us from
the evil one."

That is a marvellous prayer. A child
can understand every word of it. But it
requires a saint to pray it perfectly. It
requires a converted man to pray it sin-

cerely at all. And it is not an exaggera-
tion to say that it contains in itself the
philosophy of man's right relation to the
Supreme Will and to the whole order of
nature—the philosophy of correspondence,
which so many centuries later was expressed, with reference to the activity of
the natural sciences, in the famous aphor-
ism of Francis Bacon—"Nature can only
be controlled by being obeyed." The
true liberation of human faculties, that
is, lies in the abandonment of all wilfulness, all foolish imperiousness; it lies in
perfect submission of will to the divine
order; and this perfect submission, so far
from leading to quietism or apathy, is to
stimulate to vigorous correspondence the
man who now knows himself to be a
fellow worker with God.

How many men during this war, who
had long given up praying, have flung
themselves on their knees and prayed,
"O merciful God, I pray Thee to keep
my Tom safe!" Truly it is a most welcome
return to prayer: and certainly we should
never cease to pray thus fervently and
thus particularly for the things that we
particularly need. Still, this is the prayer
of nature, and a great interval separates
it from the prayer of enlightened sonship,
the prayer in which our personal wants

are deliberately taken up into the large scope of the Lord's Prayer.

People often ask—May we pray for rain? May we pray for this and that? I fancy the answer is fairly simple. There is one prayer which is one day going to receive its perfect answer. That is the prayer of Christ. In that we are called to share. We may pray with perfect confidence for what we know to be included in that prayer. We cannot pray at all for what we know not to be God's will, as that we should sin and not be punished, or that those we love should be blessed without being converted. But there is a vast middle region of uncertainty, a region in which we do not really know what God's will is: and in all this vast region we should let God know our desires and wishes, confessing our blindness, and imitating the wonderful humility of our Lord Himself. For He prayed "Father, if it be possible, let this cup pass from me; nevertheless, not my will but thine be done"; and was after all truly content not to be spared, not to have His natural human desire granted.

On the basis of this great principle of prayer, it is worth while to say something about (1) the different kinds of prayer, and (2) the chief aids to prayer.

1. We accept it as a natural principle
that we should begin the day with prayer.
"O Lord, in the morning shalt Thou
hear my voice: in the morning will I
order my prayer unto Thee"[1]—that is,
I will set out in order before the face of
God the day that is coming, and "will look
out" for an answer. It is natural also to
end the day with prayer—thanksgiving,
and self-examination, and confession, and
self-commendation to God. Such prayer,
the first and last thing each day, is the
most elementary provision for keeping
our life in the way of God. As the
man grows in the practice of prayer, he
will come nearer to the "seven times
a day will I praise Thee." But from the
beginning our prayer must not be selfish.
There must be intercession, at whatever
hour is most convenient. And because
a reasonably open-minded Christian has
many objects to pray for outside his own
family—as the whole of Christendom, the
evangelization of the world, the Church
in England, the clergy, his own parish, his
own profession, school, and college, the
various classes in society, the tempted and
suffering and sick—so he will have some
method of praying by which he will on
each day in the week make his interces-

[1] Ps. v. 3.

sion for some one or more of these manifold districts in the kingdom of God.
Also he will constantly remember that,
besides asking, his devotion to God should
take the form of adoration and quiet
repose upon God, and the deliberate expression of thankfulness and praise.

At the altar the Christian should find
the centre of his life of devotion. There
in the service of Holy Communion are all
kinds of prayer—penitence, and devout
reception of the word of God, and profession of faith, and intercession, and adoration of God in heaven, and thanksgiving or
eucharist, and the welcome of God incarnate brought down to earth, amongst His
worshipping people, that they may adore
"the Lamb of God which taketh away
the sins of the world," and bring all their
prayers under the shelter of His sacrifice.
There, as the climax of all, they receive
Him into themselves, and make to God
the glad return of their own lives and wills,
being joined in one with the sacrifice of
their Lord. And all the moods of this
divine worship are meant to spread from
the centre of this great common action
over all the parts of human life. Thus no
household, which aspires to become Christian, should be without some sort of family
prayers to consecrate the home. But also

praying should become the familiar expression of the soul to God, which needs
no special solitude or fixed occasion or
attitude of body, but can speak to God
anywhere in the vacant spaces of a busy
life.

2. We all find prayer very difficult. It
is difficult because it is the highest occu-
pation of man, and not therefore to be
easily learned. "No man can hope to
make progress in prayer who does not
set about it as a great work." Thus we
all suffer from wandering thoughts. But
I think the following hints may be useful
for the beginner. (1) Concentration in
prayer is greatly helped if we study concentration in all kinds of work. One who
will learn forcibly to concentrate himself
on an unwelcome piece of work will
much more easily learn to concentrate on
prayer. (2) The beginning of our prayer
is specially important, whether public or
private. We should begin by putting ourselves with all possible solemnity and
recollection into the presence of God, in
the name of Christ and in the power of
the Spirit. (3) We should intermingle in
prayer the "practice of quiet." We should
learn to abide silent and adoring in God's
presence. (4) We should vary our attitude.
Standing is quite as recognized an attitude

for prayer as kneeling. (5) We should never pray as if we were alone, or as if we were initiating a new action. There is one prayer which is always going on— it is the prayer of Christ our high priest and the intercession of the Holy Spirit, who dwells in the church, which is Christ's body, and joins in one and interprets all the prayers of all His members.

Thus whenever we begin to pray we should remember this. There is one prayer which is always being prayed— the prayer of the great High Priest and of all His people, joined together in His Spirit. Mary is praying, and Peter and Paul and John, and all the blessed dead, and all the living all the world over. Above me and around me is this mighty prayer, which is one day going to be fully answered. That will be the day of God. Meanwhile it never ceases; and every feeble prayer of mine is joined to that great stream, which fills up all my silences, and supplies all the gaps of my wandering thoughts, and interprets and perfects all my ignorant and imperfect supplications.

May God, who has given us "a hearty desire to pray," and who is "able to do more than either we desire or deserve," who also knows our weakness and ignor-ance and wilfulness, so discipline and guide and encourage us as that we may persevere and make good progress along the road of prayer: and may He at last crown our experience with this assurance—"Praised be the Lord who hath not cast out my prayer, nor turned His mercy from me."

CHAPTER VIII

The Bible—its truth, its inspiration, and its use

THERE is no doubt that the aim of the reformers of the sixteenth century, including such moderate men as Colet and Erasmus, was to make the Christian religion scriptural again—to bring back its theology to the standard of Holy Scripture, and to familiarize with Scripture the minds of all its members. This would have been a return to the earliest tradition and practice ; for the Church literature of the first four or five centuries is saturated in Scripture. There was the court of constant reference alike for its theology and its practical life. Thence was the staple of its preaching. Though there were, of course, no printed books, manuscript books were very cheap ; and Christians were exhorted and expected to buy and read the Scriptures for themselves. They are as necessary to the Christian artisan, says Chrysostom, as the tools of his trade.

It was to this tradition, then, that the
reformers sought to recall us; and with
a large measure of success. The Bible
has been the strength of English religion,
both of our learned divinity and of our
popular devotion, and has largely moulded
our national character. But our faith in
the Bible had taken the form of a belief
in the infallibility of all its statements;
and of late years this has received a rude
shock. It is not only that science seems to
make it impossible to believe that the
Bible gives us an accurate account of
the origin of the world and of our race;
it is not only that anthropology seems
to assimilate the traditions and religions rites of Israel to those of other
nations; it is not only that much which
had been believed to be historical in the
Old Testament now seems to be legen-
dary; but criticism has also assailed and
attempts to dissolve the New Testament
and the figure of the Redeemer Himself.
This destructive criticism has had its chief
origin and home in Germany, but it has
its distinguished exponents in France and
in England also. And many of our learned
men, even clergymen and professors of
theology, have published conclusions about
the New Testament which seem to simple
people to destroy the foundation of our

religion, and to plunge their minds into uncertainty and confusion. Thus it is that English popular religion, largely identified with belief in the infallibility of the Bible, has received a great shock. It is commonly supposed that "the Bible has been proved not to be true."

No doubt the faith of Roman Catholics has been less affected than that of ourselves or of the Protestant world generally; because they had practically been much less interested in the Bible and much less acquainted with it, and their faith had rested almost solely on the infallibility of the church. Now all intelligent Christian faith should rest upon the church, and not merely upon the books of the Bible; and, indeed, it should put the church before the books; because, as a matter of fact, the church existed and bore witness to the faith before the books were written. The earliest Christian books—S. Paul's Epistles—are themselves the best proof that the church was there before them, and was witnessing to the faith. Any one who reads the Epistles can see that what is substantially the faith of the Apostles' Creed was already taken for granted as the teaching of the apostles and the faith "once for all delivered to the saints," before any of the books of the New Testament were written.

Nevertheless, we will not desert the way of the ancient catholic church and the way of our own tradition. We will not allow the Bible to be dethroned or ignored or neglected. The church has given us the books of the New Testament as containing in its most authentic and inspired form the teaching of its great apostles, and has exhorted us to enlighten our minds and to preserve the purity of our religion by constant reference to the authority of these scriptures, and constant familiarity with their pages. Any ignoring or neglecting of the Bible leads assuredly to the deterioration of our religious tradition and religious life.

THE BOOKS OF THE NEW TESTAMENT

Let us, then, consider without any shrinking from the light of modern knowledge, how things stand to-day with these Holy Scriptures; and let us begin with the epistles of the New Testament, because amongst them are the earliest written documents of our religion.

Well then, after all the immense and minute attention, much of it markedly hostile attention, given to the Epistles, we can still read them as the church has given them to us, as the authentic writings of those by whom they profess to be written, with the single, not very material, exception of the Second Epistle of S. Peter.[1] That epistle is edifying indeed. But there certainly are strong reasons for doubting whether it was written by Simon Peter the apostle. As for the rest, the authenticity of no one of them has been disproved or seriously shaken: and the tendency of critical inquiry has been markedly in the conservative direction.

Side by side with these epistles you will read the history of the church in the Acts of the Apostles. No triumph of an old tradition in the world of free criticism is so marked as the triumph of the church tradition about the third Gospel and the Acts of the Apostles. After the most prolonged assaults, and the despair of many of their faint-hearted friends, these two

[1] I do not think that the ordinary man need be troubled about the authenticity of the Pastoral Epistles. The doubts seem to me to concern their style rather than their matter. It is very likely that S. Paul was more helped by some one else in writing them than in the case of his other epistles.

The Epistle to the Hebrews is anonymous. But it was written by some one of high standing in the church before the destruction of the temple at Jerusalem.

U

volumes have been, by linguistic and
historical argument, triumphantly vindicated as the trustworthy work of Luke,
the beloved physician, the companion of
S. Paul.   The Church could not have
had a better recorder of the acts of the
apostles.   He had been the personal companion of the leading apostle; and for
the earlier period, before he personally
came upon the scene, he had unrivalled
opportunities for gathering information
from those who were intimately concerned
in the earlier scenes, such as Philip the
Evangelist, one of the seven, with whom
in S. Paul's company he stayed at Caes-
area,[1] and doubtless many others.   So you
will read the Acts—surely a fascinating
book—and it will reinforce the impres-
sions of the apostolic epistles.

We are often told that the faith of the
church, as it is represented in the Epistles,
is no doubt in substance the faith of the
later catholic church; but that it is an
accretion upon the earlier faith, and the
faith of the earliest disciples is better
represented in the first three (called the
Synoptic) Gospels.   But in truth the
Synoptic Gospels only represent a faith in
process of being formed.   They are not
really intelligible apart from what they

[1] Acts xxi. 8.

led up to. They only give the account of
how the faith which is represented in the
Epistles really grew.

This makes it of the greatest importance for any intelligent study of the New
Testament that we should realize that the
Gospels were not the first of the books.
The church, after Pentecost, was worshipping the living and glorified Christ,
was living with thankfulness and courage
in the fellowship of His Spirit, was cele-
brating His atoning death and glorious
resurrection, and was confessing the
threefold name of the Father, the Son, and
the Holy Spirit, as is represented in the
Epistles. And in this atmosphere questions and anxieties and conflicts arose, and
the apostles sought to deal with the
difficulties, as appears in the Epistles,
before ever the church possessed written
Gospels. But the Twelve can never
have ceased to brood on their earlier
experiences; and, from the beginning,
they must have imparted their memories
to others, and the disciples must have
learned about the earthly life of Him
whom they now worshipped as their
Saviour and Lord. Then there would
have been, doubtless, as S. Luke says
there were, many early attempts to set
down in writing those reminiscences of

the apostolic witnesses.　For witness was
their business.　When it became necessary
to choose a successor to Judas the traitor,
S. Peter, in the days before Pentecost,
emphasizes their position as witnesses:
"Of the men therefore which have com-
panied with us all the time that the Lord
Jesus went in and went out among us,
beginning from the baptism of John, unto
the day that He was received up from us,
of these must one become a witness with us
of His resurrection"[1]—that is to say, the
official witness to the resurrection was to
be one also qualified by intimate association
with the previous life of our Lord.

Of this apostolic witness we have the
record in the Gospels.　The second of
these is the earliest; and there is every
reason for accepting the attribution of it
to S. Mark—that is to John Mark, the
companion of Paul and Barnabas, then
of Barnabas by himself, then of S. Paul
in his captivity, and later of S. Peter at
Rome, who calls him "my son."[2]　He had
himself been brought up at Jerusalem,
where his mother's house had been the
haunt of the apostles; and he probably
refers to himself in his narrative of the
passion as the young man with a linen
garment.　A sub-apostolic writer about

[1] Acts i. 22, 23.　　　[2] 1 S. Pet. v. 13.

the gospels describes S. Mark as S. Peter's interpreter, who, having constantly heard him, wrote down as accurately as possible what S. Peter used to teach. Is not such a man a good witness? And when we read the Gospel does it not force upon us the sense of reality? Is not this narrative altogether beyond human invention? Is not this the very Christ? Of course I know that a multitude of critics have in various ways sought to impugn the historical character of its various incidents. But then these critics approach their task with a strong bias, having determined that there can occur no real miracles, so that they are bound to reject any strictly miraculous incidents. This, no doubt, plays havoc with the narrative. For it is miraculous through and through. A critic of the Gospels who refuses miracles is bound to be revolutionary.

But why should we entertain such a negative dogma? If we really believe that God, the creator and sustainer of the world, has, for love of man, entered into human life in the person of Jesus Christ to redeem us, is not such a strictly re-creative act of God in itself miraculous —that is to say, is it not a fresh act of God, which the ordinary order of the world cannot account for? Is it not credible

indeed that this divine-human person
should have miraculous powers? And,
in the Gospel narrative, are not the
miracles enwrought with the teaching so
as to be of one indissoluble piece? And
does not the person Himself carry with
Him the stamp of divine authority?[1] This
is not really a matter for historical criticism. Such criticism can confirm the
tradition that the second Gospel was
really written by John Mark, who had
the best opportunities of the best information. It can assure us further that
the narrative has all the appearance of
naïve truthfulness. All this it does, and
beyond this it cannot go. It is for every
man to decide for himself whether he
will accept the witness. But when we are
considering the qualifications for forming
a judgement, we cannot help recalling the
words of our Lord, "I thank thee, Father,
Lord of heaven and earth, because thou
hast hid these things from the wise and
prudent, and hast revealed them unto
babes." The pre-occupation of the mind
with an intellectual idea, the prejudice
of the learned, may be as great an obstacle

[1] For recent discussions of miracles see Headlam's
Miracles of the New Testament (Murray); Illingworth's
Gospel Miracles (Macmillan); and Box's *The Virgin
Birth of Jesus* (Pitman).

as pride or worldliness to the obedience of Christ and the admission of the gift of faith into the soul.

Next to S. Mark's Gospel comes S. Luke's. As I have said, the vindication of S. Luke, in the face of destructive criticism, has been one of the most notable features of modern historical research. The most learned critic in Europe, Adolph Harnack, has abandoned his older opinions and come round to be a strenuous advocate of S. Luke's authorship both of the Gospel and of the Acts. In particular the historical background of S. Luke's writings has been wonderfully vindicated by actual discoveries of inscriptions and of a papyrus-leaf containing a census-paper exactly corresponding with S. Luke's description of the method of the census. His statement, "This was the first enrolment (or census) made when Quirinius was governor of Syria. And all went to enrol themselves, every one to his own city,"[1] used, when I was young, to be the common object of mockery by the critics. But you have only to read Sir William Ramsay[2] to-day to see how historical research has justified S. Luke.

[1] S. Luke ii. 2-3.
[2] *The Bearings of Recent Discovery on the Trustworthiness of the New Testament* (Hodder & Stoughton), capp. 18 ff.

Now let us read S. Luke's preface to his Gospel: "Forasmuch as many have taken in band to draw up a narrative concerning those matters which have been fulfilled among us, even as they delivered them unto us, which from the beginning were eye - witnesses and ministers of the word, it seemed good to me also, having traced the course of all things accurately from the first, to write unto thee in order, most excellent Theophilus, that thou mightest know the certainty concerning the things wherein thou wast instructed."

This is a simple and honest enough account of his motives and his methods. You may take it at its face-value; and among the previous writings which he used we must reckon S. Mark's Gospel, and probably a document which in its original form has vanished, but which was the work of S. Matthew, and con- sisted in the main of our Lord's discourses, as they appear both in S. Luke and in the first Gospel. Besides this, S. Luke had other sources of information. Names mentioned incidentally in his narrative, such as "Joanna, the wife of Chuza, Herod's steward," sometimes indicate such sources. And the narrative of our Lord's birth and infancy can have come from no other source than the circle of Mary, His mother.

What I have attempted to do so far is simply to indicate up to a certain point what sort of material historical criticism, properly so called, puts into our hands. It is quite true that a great many historical critics are rationalistic in belief, and are therefore bound to explain away all that contradicts their rationalism. But they have not all been rationalists; and some of those who have been most rationalistic have also been honest and thorough students; thus I have tried to show that we need not be afraid of their properly historical research. By far the greater part of the New Testament is given back to us with the church tradition simply verified.

As to the Gospel which bears the name of S. Matthew, I could not say the same. The bulk of it consists of the material of S. Mark's Gospel and of the collection, mainly of our Lord's discourses, made by S. Matthew. And the book as a whole plainly comes from the period before the destruction of Jerusalem, A.D. 70. But there are reasons against our ascribing it as it stands to S. Matthew's hand, and who compiled it we cannot tell. It may rightly be described as "the Gospel

according to S. Matthew" as his collection
is what specially distinguishes it ; and the
instinct of the church has made this the
premier Gospel, regarding it as giving us
the fullest narrative of our Lord's words
and acts.

As to S. John's Gospel, there has been
and is much controversy. I can only state
my conviction that those great scholars
are right who point out to us that the
evidence concerning this Gospel, internal
and external, is quite incompatible with
any other authorship except that of S. John
the apostle, "the disciple whom Jesus
loved." And this has been the assured
church tradition from the first.

In order that no one of the books may
be passed over, I must add a word about
the Revelation or Apocalypse of S. John,
that mystical book of the spiritual conflict,
so full of encouragement in the present
dark hour. Biblical criticism of recent
years has been deeply occupied in apocalyptic literature, and has shed no little
light on this, the greatest of the apocalypses.
But it has not required us in any way to
lower the traditional estimate of the book,
which claims more than any other book
of the New Testament personal inspiration for its author.

Thus, with exceptions that are really

unimportant, we may take the books of
the New Testament as they are given
us in the tradition of the church, with
the assurance that it is those who contra-
dict rather than those who affirm who do
violence to the evidence. The church
puts them into our hands as representing
the witness and mind of the first repre-
sentatives of Christ, and the freshest and
highest inspiration of His Spirit. We
shall not indeed find in the records minute
accuracy as to either our Lord's words
and works or the actions or words of
the apostles. The difference between the
forms in which the different narratives
reproduce the same incident makes this
quite evident. There are, no doubt, discrepancies. S. Chrysostom, one of the
greatest of the Fathers, was content to
recognize that the discrepancies do not
touch the main features of the portrait, and
that they guarantee to us the independence
of the witnesses. Certainly the compilers
of "memoirs of our Lord" and acts of
His apostles show no desire for minute
accuracy. But we can rely upon them
as truthful narrators and compilers who
had thoroughly trustworthy sources of
information.

But I have said all this for a strictly
practical purpose. I have sought to re-

move a preliminary obstacle to the practical
and spiritual use of the New Testament.
I have sought to give "the ordinary
person" reassurance as to the effect of
learned research. But it is the practical
use of the New Testament that I want
him to recover. What I would advise
him to do is to get a Revised Version of
the Bible, which, if it often fails in the
New Testament to retain the music of
the old version, is undoubtedly more
accurate; and I would have him put
himself to school with each book in turn,
praying first for the help of the Holy Spirit
—that is, seeking to "read the books in
the same spirit in which they were
written." I would have him read each
book through once or twice so as to
grasp its general drift, and then in due
course ponder over each passage or section, leaving out what he cannot understand, at least at first, and dwelling most
on what strikes his own conscience and
heart; and thus to "read, mark, learn, and
inwardly digest" the word of God.

I believe that there is literally nothing
in the world which is more effective for
keeping our own life in the light of God,
and for maintaining the level of the whole
church's life, than the enlightenment
which results from this sort of familiarity

on the part of all, clergy and laity alike, with "the message of the books." And, if I may judge by my own experience, the longer one pursues this sort of devout study the more convinced he will become both that the writers of the books were men inspired by the Spirit of Christ, and that in the records of Christ we have the fulfilment of His promise: "The Holy Spirit, whom the Father will send in my name, He shall teach you all things, and bring to your remembrance all that I said unto you."[1]

THE OLD TESTAMENT

No doubt the progress of science and of historical inquiry do require of us a somewhat revolutionary change from that estimate of the Old Testament in which our parents were brought up—the estimate which was derived both from the me-diaeval and from the Puritan tradition. It was claimed that the inspiration of the Bible made all its statements infallibly true, and that what is there recorded certainly happened as it is set down. This is, I think, unbelievable by any one who is at all familiar either with science or primitive history. But if this particular

[1] S. John xiv. 26.

claim made for the books of the Old
Testament is a mistaken claim, it does
not the least follow that we have not in
those books both something of the deepest
religious value and something which is
most certainly the product of divine inspiration. I believe that if we are faithful
both to reason and to religion, the use and
estimate of the Old Testament to which
we shall be led is not something quite
novel, but is closely akin to a use and
estimate of it which was widely familiar
in the early church.

The early church knew the value of
fact, and treasured the certainty of the
Gospel of fact. But it knew also, through
the Greeks, that a part of human education is due to stories which are not
true in fact, but which contain a true
moral. And it was prepared to apply this
principle of "allegory" to the Old Testament. Thus of one of the oldest of the
church Fathers, S. Irenaeus, it is recorded
that he argued for the "spiritual" (or
allegorical), as against the "historical" or
"literal" interpretation of the story of
the temptation in Genesis iii ; and a later
father, S. Gregory of Nyssa, speaks of the
same narrative as containing "doctrines
in the form of a story." It is something
like this way of regarding the opening

stories of the Bible that we want to popularize again.

Let us be quite frank. It is a mistake to look for accurate scientific information in the story of the creation or of Paradise or of the fall or of the flood. These are stories such as all primitive peoples form to embody their childlike speculations about the origin of the world. Doubtless the people of Israel shared such stories with their neighbours ; but the point is that, whereas among their neighbours these stories were full of polytheism and falsehood, in Israel the Holy Spirit of God inspired the minds of the prophets through which they passed, purged them of evil, and made them vehicles of the loftiest teaching about God, about man's nature and destiny, about the nature of sin, about divine judgement, and about God's purpose of redemption, all conveyed in the childish stories with a most impressive majesty. Really there ought to be no great difficulty in realizing that the change of view asked of us is no spiritual loss at all, and that it is not the purpose of inspiration to teach us science.

Again, our fathers were brought up to believe that (if I may so speak) Almighty God constructed in His own mind the elaborate law of worship which is contained in Exodus and Leviticus, and gave it in so many words to Moses, who instituted it. This is the form which Jewish reverence for the Law as divine had given to the narrative. But the early Christian church knew that all these elements of ritual were shared by the Jews with their heathen neighbours: that they all "had their origin," as Chrysostom expresses it, "from Gentile grossness." They would not have been in the least shocked by anything which the comparative study of primitive religions has taught us about the Jewish ceremonial. They were as eager as possible to see in the Jewish law an instance of God's gradual method of education, by which He takes men as He finds them, with all manner of savage customs and rites, and gradually brings them under a discipline which at last shall enable them to dispense with their barbarous rudiments and be ready for a spiritual religion. It would be very easy to quote the Christian Fathers to this effect one after another.

Again, many of the Fathers had not the least difficulty in recognizing in the moral discipline of the Israelites an instance of the same gradual method. "God," they said, "condescended to allow and even to command what He is far from finally approving, in order to avoid worse things and to lead men on to better."

In fact, the minds of many of the Fathers were full of this principle of a gradual discipline for men—a gradual leading from barbarism up to a spiritual level—and they applied this principle freely to the Old Testament. The chief instrument of this divine leading was prophecy. In the teaching of the Hebrew prophets they discerned "the sacred school of the knowledge of God and of the spiritual life for all mankind." I believe that this great saying of S. Athanasius contains the most profound insight into the Old Testament. Every divine vocation or special election of any man or body of men is for the sake of all mankind. As the Greeks for art and intellect, as the Romans for order and empire, so the Hebrews had a divine vocation for religion, and that for the sake of all mankind. The Jewish prophets were men specially susceptible of religion, who were chosen as the special vehicles and instruments of the divine Spirit. They were allowed to feel and know the will of God. They truly spoke the word of the Lord—His message to the people of Israel, and so indirectly to mankind at large.

I believe that nothing is more morally certain than that those prophets, from Samuel, Elijah, and Elisha down to the second Isaiah and Malachi, were really inspired, really enabled to receive and to utter the message of God, through a number of centuries and under great variation of circumstance and temperament, but with marvellous consistency, till the great spiritual doctrine about God and man, which we owe to the Jews, and which is the basis of the catholic religion, was formed and accepted as divine in the heart of the whole people. And this spiritual doctrine which was uttered by the prophets gradually reformed the thoughts of Israel, inspiring their stories of the beginning of the world, inspiring their national legends, inspiring their history, moulding their traditional ritual to express a spiritual purpose, controlling their speculation, as in Job and Ecclesiastes, giving tone to their practical wisdom, as in Proverbs and the like books, expressing itself in the profound religious feeling of the psalms of the sanctuary, inspiring also later "stories with a moral," like Esther, Jonah, and the stories of the Book of Daniel—all no doubt based on a historical tradition—above all expressing itself in the certain anticipation of the Day of the Lord and the appearance of the divine Christ. Can we not learn to take this view of the Old Testament? It is in most thorough harmony with the great words in which the New Testament writers expound to us the purpose of the Old Testament.

"God having of old times spoken unto the fathers in the prophets by divers portions and in divers manners, hath at the end of these days spoken unto us in his Son."[1] "Whatsoever things were written aforetime were written for our learning, that through patience and encouragement of the scriptures we might have hope."[2] "Every scripture inspired of God is also profitable for teaching, for reproof, for correction, for instruction in righteousness, that the man of God may be complete, furnished completely unto every good work."[3] In fact, if a man will take such a modern and scientific interpreter of the Old Testament as Dr. Driver or Dr. George Adam Smith, or Dr. Robertson Smith, and really enter into his spirit, I think he will be brought to believe in the inspiration of the writers of the Old Testament as he never believed in it before, and will experience a constantly deepened conviction that "salva-

[1] Heb. i. 1.   [2] Rom. xv. 4.   [3] 2 Tim. iii. 16-17.

tion was of the Jews "—that they were the divinely chosen nursery of the catholic religion, and that the divine Spirit really did inspire their prophets and mould their institutions to prepare the way for the Christ.[1]

And must it not be said at this moment of the war that our interest in the Old Testament has been marvellously deepened and intensified by our experiences? Have we ever felt the Psalms or the Prophets as we have felt them the last two years? Do we not know, as we never knew it before, that they are the faithful interpreters of the judgements and purposes of God?

The Bible in all its parts is the record of God's revelation of Himself. It embodies and conveys to us His word. May He, who by the entrance of His word gives light to the soul, help us with the Spirit of understanding, that being taught of Him in His Holy Scriptures we may understand the words of eternal life and be made wise unto salvation!

[1] The most useful commentary of a comprehensive kind for the beginner to have at hand is, I think, Dummelow's *One Volume Bible Commentary* (Macmillan).

CHAPTER IX

The Church of England in the Larger World

1. THE OTHER PARTS OF CHRISTENDOM

I HAVE tried to expound the religion of the church and of the Bible—saying nothing, I trust, that our special Anglican formulas do not admit of, but endeavouring to speak as one who remembers that our Church of England and the whole Anglican communion is only a portion of a larger whole which embraces and controls it. What I believe in is not the Church of England but the one holy catholic church. But unfortunately this one holy catholic church has, as far as this world is concerned, fallen into divisions; and I must say something about the relation of the Church of England to other parts of a divided Christendom.

Thus, first we find ourselves confronted with the great church of the Roman communion which, since we repudiated the authority of the Roman pontiff in the

sixteenth century, superciliously repudi-
ates our claim to be part of the catholic
church at all, and claims to be by itself
alone the one holy catholic church.
Superciliousness, however, and contemp-
tuous ignoring of others are not always
marks of a true claim. [1]

So far as concerns the claim of the
Church of Rome to be the whole church,
we had better leave it to be dealt with
by the Eastern and Russian churches,
which are likely to bulk bigger on the
horizon of the West in the future. There
is not in truth any sound reason at all
in the Roman attempt to ignore the great
Eastern communion. That has simply and
persistently maintained its ancient position.
The church of the great Greek fathers has
all along steadily repudiated the claim
of the Bishop of Rome to be by divine
appointment the necessary head of the
catholic church, and all the accompanying dogmatic and disciplinary claims.
It has steadily refused to alter its position.
And, as I said, this Russian and Eastern
Christendom is too great to be ignored.
It is like a vast breakwater, meeting and
throwing back the Roman claim long
before it reaches us. It simply disposes
of the demand of the Roman communion

[1] Ezek. xvi. 44–63 is very instructive.

to be regarded as the whole church. But more than that, it represents a type of catholicism strangely and deeply different from the Roman type.[1] It establishes the invaluable principle that catholicism is a comprehensive thing, admitting of different national and racial types, all of which are necessary for the full development of the religion of Christ. And if it be once granted that the Eastern and Russian church is as legitimate and regular a part of the church (to say the least) as the Church of Rome, I do not think that we in our turn shall find it difficult to maintain our position. If there is a providence to be seen in history anywhere, its action is surely apparent in the circumstances which have given to our Anglican communion its special character and vocation in Christendom. The ancient catholic church had four outward and visible bonds of unity universally accepted : there was the tradition of the faith to be maintained, which was embodied in the catholic creeds and dogmatic definitions of the undivided church ; there was the system of the sacraments ; there was the due succession of the bishops ; and there were the Scriptures, the inspired books of the

[1] See *Lectures on the Russian Church* (S.P.C.K., 1915). "Its doctrine." By W. J. Birkbeck.

church, the constant ground of appeal in matters of doctrine and the perpetual standard of spiritual life.

All these elements of catholic communion we, in the providence of God, have retained through all periods of peril and weakness; the last we have restored to its true position. The appeal to Scripture and antiquity [1] as limiting and restraining the dogmatic power of the church is unmistakably the principle of the ancient church; and, if it be accepted, it prevents the accumulation of dogma beyond the limits of the original doctrine. The church has no other dogmatic function but to protect, interpret, and hand on the "faith once for all delivered to the saints." This is the safeguard of liberty and comprehensiveness. Thus we stand, over against Rome, a part of the catholic church which has repudiated nothing that is properly authoritative, seeking to embody a catholicism true to history and Scripture and to the ancient liberties of Christendom; treating Roman Christianity with

[1] The Holy Scriptures stand as a court of appeal distinct from antiquity, in virtue of the special inspiration and authority of the writers. This is unmistakably the case in the mind of the great Christian fathers. But in fact there is not, as far as I know, any doctrine which can fairly claim the support of antiquity as being part of the faith, which is not also plainly in the New Testament.

the respect and reverence which it deserves, but as a one-sided development of catholicism—a development which, in accordance with the natural genius of Rome, has over-emphasized and exaggerated the dogmatic and governmental elements in the church at the expense both of liberty and of truth; consistently making our appeal behind the middle ages to the ancient and undivided church and to Scripture. And if we are wise we shall never imagine that we can, in admiration of Roman efficiency, seek to acclimatize amongst ourselves the Roman system without the Pope. The whole ecclesiastical development in the West during the later middle age and subsequently has centred in the papacy, and is of one piece with it. And if we are not intending to submit to the Pope on his own terms, we must in all respects seek to maintain and build up our system on the principles of the ancient church and the holy Scriptures.

But we are confronted also with the "Free churches," the churches that are frankly Protestant. Now it is impossible to deny or ignore the fact that, whereas the Anglican church, in its reformation, carefully maintained the properly catholic tradition in structure and doctrine of the

z

undivided church, the Protestant churches
of the continent and of Scotland definitely
did not.   The Reformation with them became a thoroughgoing rebellion against the
old church, and in particular a repudiation of the ancient ministry.   The succession which we retained they repudiated.
Thus in claiming (with Luther) that each
group of " faithful " Christians could appoint and ordain its own ministers, or
(with Calvin) that, owing to the apostasy
of the ancient priesthood, God had origin-
ated a new ministry, they were alike
definitely rebelling not only against particular laws, but also against a fundamental
principle of the ancient church.   The same
thing has been true of the later-formed
"nonconformist" bodies ; and it follows
that we could not accept their ministers
as validly ordained ministers, or   their
sacramental ministrations as valid ministrations, without cutting off ourselves with
them from the fellowship of the ancient
church, and from all hope of reunion on
a catholic basis, for   instance, with the
Eastern   and   Russian   church.   There
seems to me to be no escape from this
conclusion.   But we can only say this with
much compunction.

We know quite well how the nonconformist bodies in England grew up.   We

know quite well under what conditions they have been recruited and gained their strength. It has been largely, at least, because of our failure to be what a church ought to be. We have by our sins and shortcomings supplied them with only too much excuse for separation. It will cause us, therefore, the less surprise to find the tokens of the action of the Holy Spirit most plainly evident among them, not only among those who in virtue of baptism are individually members of the church, but quite as obviously among the Quakers and elsewhere where baptism is rejected. We know how often the zeal and holiness of individual nonconformists puts us to shame, and we know too how often the spirit of brotherhood and the " preparedness of the gospel of peace " have been found in their organizations when they have been sadly lacking in ours. I am sure we ought to recognize, as frankly as possible, that God has been pleased to work with a full measure of His grace far beyond all normal channels and laws of validity. I trust that the attitude of contempt which is so common in Romanists towards us, and has been so common, alas ! in Anglicans towards nonconformists, will become very rapidly a thing of the past. I trust we shall learn to hold with them the fullest measure

of Christian fellowship which we can hold
without faithlessness to the principles we
stand for.   And if I am asked whether in
making such admissions as these I am not
practically abandoning my principles, I dare
to reply with a very emphatic denial.

Whatever apology the shortcomings and
abuses of the church make for Protestantism, I cannot but feel that Protestantism—
whether it be considered as a Christianity
which seeks to stand upon the Bible
divorced from the authority of the church,
or as a repudiation of the sacramental
system, or as an appeal from the visible to
an invisible church, or as a repudiation of
the apostolic succession—is less and less
able to justify itself by an appeal to original
Christianity, and bears with increasing
plainness the appearance of a temporary
rebellion which lacks in itself the conditions of reconstruction and permanence.

It has become, for instance, increasingly
evident that the Bible will not stand as
a basis of doctrine divorced from the
authority of the visible church.   But something much larger is also becoming evident.
There is a growing disgust with our divisions, both the divisions in our national
Christianity and the divisions between
national churches.   These, it is widely
felt, have in effect destroyed the moral

force which the catholic church as a super-
national society — holding all nations together on the basis of a wider fellowship —
was intended to exercise. But if the desire
for this catholic fellowship should really
revive among the nations, if we should
begin again seriously to consider afresh
that our Lord willed us all to be one in a
visible church, nothing surely is more certain than that the only possible road to
reunion will be found to be upon the basis
of the ancient catholic tradition.

The spirit and meaning of that tradition
I have tried to describe. The idea of the
visible church, the idea of the sacraments,
the idea of the ministerial succession, cohere as indissoluble elements in one idea
and one institution. And this idea and
institution cohere in turn with the incarnation. Thus—Christ is the embodiment of
God. God was, and is, at work in the
world outside the incarnate Christ: but
as soon as Christ has been presented to
us we cannot reject Him and still keep
our hold on God. So the visible church
is the embodiment of Christ—the extension of the incarnation; and, as soon as
the church is really presented to us, we
cannot reject the church and still hold
Christ. "As the Father hath sent me, even
so send I you." "He that heareth you

heareth me ; and he that rejecteth you rejecteth me ; and he that rejecteth me, rejecteth him that sent me."[1] The same principle unites Christ to God and the church to Christ. It is the manifestation of God in a definite visible form. It is exactly this principle as applied to the church which Protestantism seems to me to reject. I think its rejection is the heart of Protestantism. Let us listen to such familiar protests as these : "I cannot believe that material things can be such necessary instruments of the gifts of the Holy Spirit." "1 cannot believe that the Holy Spirit can wait upon the ministrations of a man who may be an unspiritual and wicked man, because he happens to have received the laying on of a bishop's hands." "I will not have a priest standing between me and God." "Surely, if my faith in Christ is real, it matters comparatively little what body of Christians I belong to, or what outward forms I use."

It is worth while spending a little time over such protests. I have no doubt that they make a strong appeal to a great many religious Englishmen. But as regards the first two protests, I would ask any one who is impressed by them to con-

[1] S. John xx. 21 ; S. Luke x. 16.

sider what is, after all, the basis of spiritual
life on earth, the way in which the human
spirit has its origin. Is any spiritual power
that a man can exercise so portentously
great or so fundamental as the power to
bring into the world an immortal soul,
a spiritual personality with its infinite
capacities? Does any power claimed for
any priesthood equal this? And is it
not an undeniable fact that in the order
of God this tremendous spiritual power is
embedded in the physical and sexual nature
of man, just at the point where the physical most easily degenerates into the sensual?
Does not this mean that God, the life-
giving Spirit, does confessedly choose to
commit Himself to physical channels and
to the will of even wicked men? Is not
the sacramental principle affirmed here,
if I may say so, in its most perilous form?
The fact is so staggering, and yet so undeniable, that it seems to me to silence once
and for all the objections which naturally
rise in our minds against the sacramental
system, on the ground of its apparent subjection of the action of the Holy Spirit to
physical methods and to the wills of men.[1]
I believe it destroys fundamentally any

[1] I say "apparent subjection" because I should not
admit that in the sacramental system there is any real
subjection. "God is not tied to the sacraments."

justification for protests against the idea of material things as channels of spiritual grace, or against the idea that "the un-worthiness of the minister does not hinder the grace of the sacraments."

God the eternal Spirit has plainly no horror of taking material means, however liable to be misused, as instruments of His spiritual action. This is strictly all the conclusion that I would draw from the above consideration. What we are to be-lieve positively about the sacraments and their conditions must depend upon what we actually find to be the message of the Gospel. But there, I contend, at the heart of the original Gospel, we find the church with its sacraments and its ministry.

As to the other familiar protests of Pro-testantism—the two last expressed above —I would say: God does mean the individual soul to have full personal communion with Him in Christ; and nowhere, in fact, has this communion been more personal or more intense than in the catholic church. But also He has willed that the individual should enter into this covenant of communion with Himself only in fellowship with other men, only as a member of a body, in due subordination to the body. Sacraments are no more oppo-site to faith than food is opposite to hunger.

But the sacraments supply the soul with its necessary nourishment in such a way as to keep it in dependence upon the body, the church. The ministry, again, if it be rightly used, no more stands "between the soul and God" than the father and mother necessarily stand between the soul and God : nor does the church as a whole "stand between the soul and God." But membership in the church is the divinely-imposed condition of the soul entering into and continuing in that communion with God which Christ came to make possible for man. And that because, at the bottom, it is the will of God that only in communion with, and in subordination to, our fellows should we be enabled to realize the end of our being.

2. CHURCH REFORM

A Church-of-England man who finds himself called upon to vindicate the position and claim of the part of the church to which he belongs can only do so with much compunction. It is not our business to compare ourselves with other parts of the church. But it is our business to be deeply conscious of our defects. And there is no denying that we have tolerated, and are tolerating, with an almost incredible

acquiescence conspicuous abuses in our
system.   That a clergyman, in virtue of
the "parson's freehold," should be allowed
manifestly to neglect his duties as a parish
priest, and to be in all respects not an
incumbent but an incubus, and still to
retain his position, defying parish and
bishop alike, so long as he does not
commit some flagrant breach of the law,
is undoubtedly a grave scandal, and it is
difficult to exaggerate the mischief done
by a few such cases in each diocese.
Again, that the right of presenting a
clergyman to the pastoral charge of a
parish should be a piece of property,
which can still be sold or bought with
lamentably little restriction, is a like
scandal, which would not be tolerated if
what were in question were a public
school mastership or a professorship.
Again, that an incumbent should be able,
owing to the collapse of ecclesiastical discipline, arbitrarily to alter the customs of
worship in a parish, almost without restraint, is another abuse which has deeply
alienated reasonable Englishmen from the
church.   But the most fundamental of all
these scandals—the cause at bottom of all
the others—is that we should have been
content and should still be content, in
defiance of the intentions of Christ and

of the spirit of the church, to suffer the Church of England to lack the power of self-government. In consequence of this loss we drag on our way with largely antiquated rules. We are constantly involved in obscure discussions as to the meaning of ancient rubrics, instead of making new canons and rules to suit our present needs. The result of such paralysis of the church's action has been a lamentable lawlessness which has infected bishops, clergy, and laity alike. An almost unrestrained individualism has taken the place of the corporate loyalty and subordination which is the mark of a healthy society. It cannot be doubted that a "converted church" would imperiously demand, at whatever cost, the restoration to it of its normal, divinely-given, power of self-government.

And in a democratic age we should seek a scheme of self-government such as will give to every element of the community, to bishops and clergy and laity alike, in each parish and diocese and in the church as a whole, its legitimate place and function in the system of government. The Christian church can never be a pure democracy. For the church is first of all a monarchy, and the will of Christ, expressed through the dogmatic and disci-

plinary authority of the church catholic, is
a law over every local or national church.
Moreover it is by the will of Christ and
the fundamental law of the church that
the hierarchy holds its proper place, and
there is entrusted to bishops and clergy
a ministry of the word and sacraments
which the body of the church has neither
conferred upon them nor can take away.
But in the early church the democratic
element in government was much more
conspicuous than in subsequent ages from
a variety of causes it became.   The
method of government in the church
naturally tends to conform itself to the
spirit and method of government which
prevails in society as a whole.   Thus
in imperialist and feudal times the democratic spirit in the government of the
church was weakened and almost lost.
But in days when democracy is the spirit
of the times the church should revive
in the whole body of the laity powers of
control both in parochial affairs and in the
church at large which have been allowed
to sleep, but have never been and never
can be abolished.   A few years ago the
archbishops appointed a committee, thoroughly representative of the various
schools of thought in the church, to consider how best the church could set itself

to recover its legitimate and inalienable function of self-government. This year (1916) this committee has reported, and its report is in the hands of the church. It is not asking too much to urge that every member of the church who wants to fulfil his function in "loosing his mother from her chains" should study this report and co-operate in a vigorous and insistent demand for the restoration of the church's liberty. I do not think that the proposals of this committee will be found to contravene any principle of catholic order. I see no other real hope for our sorely crippled and weakened church than that it should resolutely set itself in correspondence with the purpose of our Lord and in obedience to His Spirit, to the task of self-reform, remembering that it is the whole church, and not only the clergy, which is the royal and priestly body, and that every member who has received the unction of the Holy Spirit in confirmation should take his part or her part in the blessed work of liberation and recovery.

3. THE EVANGELIZATION OF THE WORLD

Of course the Church of England, like every part of the church, must refuse to be content with its home concerns, and

must take its place in the fulfilment of
a world-wide mission—"Go ye into all the
world, and make disciples of all the
nations." To-day in the political field we
Englishmen have to learn the duties and
opportunities which a world-wide empire
lays upon us. We have to organize the
empire for the fulfilment of its mission.
And in the religious sphere our empire,
in India and Africa, lays upon us a very
special obligation for bringing to the non-
Christian peoples who are our fellow
subjects not only such secular advantages
as their fellowship in our empire ought to
confer, but the opportunity of that deeper
fellowship which only the catholic gospel
can bestow. But the obligation to evan-
gelize the world is far wider than the
empire. It is an obligation to China and
Corea and Japan as well as to India.

No doubt "missionary work" has made
great advances among us. We no longer talk
of its being "better to leave the heathen to
their own religions." We understand that
such a policy is not only faithlessness to
Christ, but also an impossibility. The
authority and discipline of the old heathen
religions is weakened inevitably by the
spread of Western science and by the min-
gling throughout the world of European
influences with native customs and modes

of thought. By our mere presence among
them we inevitably tend to destroy the old
religions. The question is, What are we
going to promote in their place? It is the
Christian church only which has an answer
to the question. It is Christianity alone
which can claim to be a catholic religion.
The obligation to assist in the evangelization of the world lies upon every one who
accepts the allegiance of Christ. To be
content to keep our religion for home con-
sumption is truly to forfeit our allegiance.
Every consistent and intelligent churchman must take his part in the spread of
the kingdom of Christ. To be narrow and
merely national in our religious sympathies
is to cease to be in any real sense Christian.

4. RELIGION AND SCIENCE

Freedom should be the spirit of the
church and not least intellectual freedom.
Freedom means that the churchman who
has really assimilated his religion should
find, as S. Paul says, that "all things are
his" — that he can feel at home in the
whole universe, as a son in the Father's
house — and this cannot be without intellectual liberty. He should be un-
shackled and open-eyed in the whole
world of investigation and discovery.

There should be no conflict between religion and science, and no restraint on free inquiry. There is, in fact, in the New Testament no trace of obscurantism, but a love of the light, without limit or boundary.

There has been, however, undoubtedly a very often renewed conflict between religion and science—using the term in its broadest sense as covering historical science and the study of the history of morality and religion, as well as the physical sciences. And the cause of it has, perhaps, been threefold.

(1) Christianity quite definitely claims that the self-revelation of God, given through the Hebrew prophets and in Christ, has pushed back the boundary of darkness, and given mankind a definite knowledge of divine things which it could not otherwise have had.

Christianity is not concerned to deny that God has given some measure of revelation of Himself among all nations; it is not concerned to minimize the elements of truth to be found among them. Quite the contrary. But it is concerned to maintain a special vocation of the Jews to be the instruments of divine revelation, and to maintain that this revelation as consummated in Christ supersedes, not only the Jewish religion, but all other religions, not by a method of exclusion, but by the inclusion in a completer whole of all the elements of truth which each contains. And this belief in a positive revelation of God consummated in Christ does exclude all manner of contradictory ideas about God, about sin, about human destiny, such as have been current among men. Christianity, for instance, must be in everlasting opposition to any religion or philosophy or school of thought which is based on pantheism, or which denies to man the real freedom of his will, as the basis of moral responsibility, or which treats sin as if it had its seat and root in our material nature instead of being a rebellion of the will, or which denies any other element in the positive revelation given in Christ. That is the point. Christianity claims that God has given to man, by revelation, a positive knowledge about God, coupled with, and involving, a positive knowledge about human nature and sin and divine redemption. This from the first made it necessary, and must for ever make it necessary, that Christianity should be a controversial religion, waging war against every idea or philosophy which would undermine

2 B

its foundation principles. It is prob-
able that these principles would never
have been discovered by the groping
of the human intellect. At any rate they
were not so discovered. Men do in fact
owe them to the Hebrew prophets and to
Christ. But, once accepted as true, they
become the basis of a philosophy which,
better than any other philosophy (so the
Christian must contend), can interpret
and co-ordinate all the facts and phases
of experience. And it is a disastrous
mistake on the part of Christian philoso-
phers to allow the world to forget what
is the real source of our knowledge of
God and of ourselves. In this sense—
that is in so far as science is using a
background of false assumptions—conflict
between religion and science is inevitable.

(2) But so far as scientific research is
using no such false assumptions, a Christian ought to enjoy the fullest freedom
in the world of knowledge. I have myself
from time to time been a respectful spec-
tator of the conversion of a man of science
from agnosticism or a very vague belief
in God to a full Christian belief. Such
conversions have come about from various
causes, intellectual or moral. But when
the Christian faith has once been frankly

accepted as "the word of God," it has been very interesting and reassuring to see that the man of science has not suffered in his scientific freedom—that, while he has found himself in corre-spondence with a new world of spiritual experiences, he has not found himself hampered or restrained in his old world of scientific research.

But it cannot be denied that it has not always been so. It cannot be denied that the church has often been really obscurantist, has often laid upon the intellect illegitimate claims, and has occasioned in intellectual circles suspicion and rebellion for which there was too much justification. The Roman church has been, no doubt, a great offender. When S. Ignatius of Loyóla bids his retreatants "always to hold the principle that the white that I see I would believe to be black, if the hierarchical church were so to rule it," [1] he is laying upon the intellect a claim which I do not think anything can justify. Wisely, with Bishop Butler, we should repudiate such a claim. We should hold that it is an important test of the divine origin of our religion that it frees us to observe all that can be observed, to examine

[1] *Spiritual Exercises*, edited by J. Rickaby, S.J. (Burns & Oates, 1915), p. 223.

all that can be examined, and to know
all that can be known by our natural
faculties in the world of God. But it
cannot be denied that we have been also
offenders against the light. We took surely
too long a time before we were ready to
recognize, even if we are quite ready to
recognize it to-day, that the early chapters
of Genesis are not to be treated as con-
veying scientific information ; and that it
is not a dogma of the faith that the books
of Jonah and Daniel are historical records.
We ridicule working people nowadays
who ask about Cain's wife. But we are
responsible for their asking the question.
We were afraid where no fear was. We
perpetuated a needless conflict between
religion and science, and we alienated a
great many honest inquirers, through being
much too slow to welcome new light.

(3) But it must not be forgotten that
a vast part of the conflict in the minds of
individuals between the claims of religious
faith, as they have inherited it, and the
conclusions of intellectual inquiry, is due
to the doubter never having really given
his faculties to the study of religion. My
grandmother Lois and my mother Eunice
were excellent teachers of spiritual lessons,
and they brought me up to know what a
Christian ought to know. But it does not

follow that I am justified in taking the lessons exactly as they taught them me out into the intellectual world, as if they were final statements of Christian doctrine. It is very strange how few well educated men and women are at all at pains really to apply their minds either to studying some rational account of their religion or, if they are able, to studying the documents of their religion for themselves. I do not think it is possible to exaggerate the difference it would make to men and women without number, if they would only give themselves the time, not without prayer, but also not without a real effort of their minds, to win for themselves a clear perception of the coherence, the solidarity, and the meaning of the articles of the Christian faith.

5. CHURCHMANSHIP AND CITIZENSHIP

Our Lord took for granted the political life of man, and said little about it. But He set to work in the world a principle of humanity which could not but have a profound effect on politics—the principle of the absolute and equal value of every human soul. At the beginnings of Christianity, under the Roman Empire, the members of the church found themselves debarred from imperial politics, though they developed fruitful principles for the regulation of their own internal life. But in time Christian states arose; and it would seem to be obvious that a community dominated by the Christian spirit must feel the obligation to legislate and fashion its institutions so as at least to facilitate and not to hinder the development of the Christian ideal of life.

The result has no doubt been very disappointing. States have been Christian in the sense that they have sought to enforce by law the profession of Christianity. But society has not been so really converted as to break the tyranny of custom and tradition, or to make the strong ashamed to prey upon the weak. On the whole Christian states, so-called, have given but a very disappointing picture of the social application of Christian principles. Especially in recent history they have too readily acquiesced in a political economy, really anti-Christian in principle, which by substituting unrestrained competition for co-operation has undermined the very basis of fellowship.

Let us take one example of this failure. In the early days Christians could not affect the laws or institutions of the empire. They could only combine to keep one another from want. Almsgiving, the relief of the needs of the poor by the rich, or of the sick by the healthy members of the community, was effective on the whole and not demoralizing; for Christians were running a common risk; the tie of brotherhood was very close; and the claim for almsgiving, according to a man's means, was accompanied by an equal insistence that each man must do his best to support himself. "If a man will not work, neither let him eat."

But when Christians gained control of legislation another duty ought to have arisen into prominence—that of so moulding the institutions of the state as to prevent pauperism and disease. It seems to be only now that we are waking up to our vast neglect in this respect. The church has constantly been occupied in picking up the wounded in the battle of life—in providing medicines and staunching wounds —when it ought to have been thundering at the gates of tyranny. It ought not to have allowed the organized forces of vice and selfishness to entrench themselves and build their castles and provide themselves with munitions. It ought to have been militant in such sense as to force men to see in it the determined and constant enemy of selfishness and wrong; it ought

to have had discernment enough to tear
the cloak of respectability off the strong-
holds of evil, and courage enough to force
men to choose, not only in their private
lives but on the public stage, between
their Christian profession and their selfish,
anti-social, claims.   Now there is no longer
in any modern state any question of
compelling men to be Christians; there
is indeed hardly any question of the
state definitely maintaining the Christian
standard as such ; but there is a great and
fresh opportunity for Christians of all
kinds to combine and show the world
what an organized Christian public opinion,
making the most of its citizenship, can
effect — a great and fresh opportunity to
make it evident that the laws and institutions which the church can support must
be laws and institutions which really embody and promote the Christian ideal of
brotherhood.

I have come to the end of what has
proved a very difficult task—that of providing within a very short compass a
comprehensive account of the Christian
religion.   A book of this kind, which
must advance so many statements without
being able to buttress them with proofs,
lays itself open to manifold criticism.

So I will venture to conclude with the words with which S. Ignatius prefaced his *Spiritual Exercises*—"It must be pre-supposed that every good Christian should be more ready to approve than to condemn a proposition advanced by his neighbour: and if he cannot approve it, let him inquire into his meaning; and if it be erroneous, let him correct him lovingly; and if that does not suffice, let him employ all suitable means that his neighbour may be brought to a right mind and stand approved."

INDEX

Printed by A. R. Mowbray & Co. Ltd., London and Oxford

CPSIA information can be obtained
at www.ICGtesting.com
Printed in the USA
BVHW061225241218
536332BV00035B/1618/P